Political Ideals

Houston Stewart Chamberlain

Translated with an Introduction and Notes by

Alexander Jacob

University Press of America,® Inc.
Dallas · Lanham · Boulder · New York · Oxford

Contents

Acknowledgements

This edition of Chamberlain's *Politische Ideale* (1915) developed as an offshoot of my researches in natural philosophy, which were consolidated in my book, *De Naturae Natura: A Study of Idealistic Conceptions of Nature and the Unconscious*, Stuttgart: Franz Steiner, 1992. Chamberlain himself moved from the study of natural science and natural philosophy to the field of political ideas, and my repetition of this sequence is only a confirmation of the intimate relation between idealistic natural philosophy and idealistic political philosophy.

Chamberlain's writings also reveal the powerful forces that were at work in Germany at the beginning of this century, and serve to explain the trends which took control following the ill-designed Treaty of Versailles and the Weimar Republic. It is to be hoped that this translation will enrich the understanding of English-speaking scholars with regard to the contrasting philosophies that motivated the European protagonists who participated in the two major world wars - wars that resulted in the political as well as cultural destruction of traditional, aristocratic Europe.

I should like to thank here the Centre for the Philosophy of Science at York University for the Fellowship that they granted me during the writing of this work.

Toronto

Alexander Jacob

Introduction

I: Houston Stewart Chamberlain (1855-1927): A Biographical Sketch

Houston Stewart Chamberlain is relatively little known to modern readers, but he played a major role in shaping attitudes and ideas in the Germany of the first half of this century, and an acquaintance with his literature, his views and his important contacts with the leaders of the Germany of this time - with Kaiser Wilhelm and with Adolf Hitler - who shared his views and were undoubtedly influenced by his philosophy, greatly helps us to appreciate the contrasting ideals which then divided Europe and were largely responsible for World War I, which in turn served as a prelude to World War II.

Chamberlain's own Germanism sprang from his identification of the Anglo-Saxon and Norman-Frankish origins of his own ancestors as members of the Germanic family of nations. His own adoption of German nationality and his glorification of Germanic traditions, values, culture and politics were born of an innate affinity with the racial values with which the German people identified at the turn of the century. These inclinations were reinforced and further cultivated through his studies of Wagner, Goethe, Kant, Stein, and, in various political tracts issued during the first Great War, he mirrored what he regarded as the ennobling cultural standards that prevailed in Germany before the two world wars plunged the country into, first, physical devastation and, then, deleterious political and cultural transformations. Reading Chamberlain is one of the best ways of understanding the idealism that inspired and strengthened the Wilhelminian Reich and the very real philosophical conflicts in the Europe of that period which were largely responsible for both the first Great War and the second. It provides, at the same time, a means of measuring the distance that separates modern Germany and the world in general from the ideals and values that inspired the major political and cultural figures of Germany a hundred years ago.

Chamberlain was born the son of a British admiral who traced his ancestry back to the Earls of Westmorland and, through them, to the Plantagenet kings of England and France.[1] This alone would in many circumstances be enough to explain his reverence for the concept of nobility of thought and action, his dedication to the ideal of romantic nationalism, and his contempt for the self-seeking and corrupt party politics characteristic of those nations governed by democratic political systems. He saw the history of Europe in terms of the Spartan aristocratic and monarchical tradition rather than the latter-day Athenian democracy when Athenian freemen were cajoled into selling their votes to wealthy alien merchants living in the port of Piraeus.

Chamberlain's mother died before Houston Stewart Chamberlain was a year old, and he and his brothers, Basil and Henry, were raised by his aunt Harriet Chamberlain in Versailles. At the age of ten, Chamberlain was enrolled in a private academy in Portsmouth, but his experiences there did not suit his extremely sensitive and solitary nature. After a brief return to France, he was sent back to England, this time to Cheltenham College, which provided a more congenial educational atmosphere. In 1869, however, Chamberlain was removed from Cheltenham to be taken care of by his aunt Harriet in the Continent, and he never again lived in England for any considerable period of time. The next nine years were spent travelling in Europe, and during this period he visited Germany for the first time in 1870. This visit left an indelible impression of both the idealistic and romantic nature of Germany as a whole and of the military prowess of Prussia, which Chamberlain in his later intellectual autobiography, described as "a heroic Germany, establishing itself with the insuperable power of right and its knightly cadres command-ed by immortal heroes."[2] Shortly after, while staying at Montreux, Chamberlain was provided with the services of a young German tutor, Otto Kuntze, who was responsible for inspiring in the English boy a fervent love of German culture. In 1874, while at Cannes, Chamber-

---

1 I am indebted in this sketch to the detailed biography of Chamberlain in Geoffrey Field, *Evangelist of Race: The Germanic Vision of Houston Stewart Chamberlain*, N.Y.: Columbia Univ. Press, 1981.
2 *Lebenswege meines Denkens*, München: F. Bruckmann, 1919, p.54 (tr. G. Field, *op.cit.*, p.28).

life force

lain met Anna Horst, a Prussian who was then earning a living as a private tutor. After a four-year long friendship, Chamberlain married Horst in 1878, although she was ten years his senior. After further travels in Italy, Chamberlain decided to move to Geneva where he enrolled in the university. He earned his baccalaureat in 1881 and proceeded to his doctorate in plant chemistry. Poor health hampered his research and he did not finish his thesis until 1896,[3] by which time he was living in Vienna. His focus was increasingly on a vitalist theory of plant physiology which assumed the existence of a life force.[4] His thesis in fact reflected Goethe's doctrine that a subjective imaginative insight into life, rather than a mere observation of the phenomena, was a prerequisite of scientific research. In short, he was already absorbed into the German idealistic tradition, then long recognized throughout Europe. Indeed, it was the French Comte de St. Simon, the originator of sociology, who had said that only the Germans were sufficiently idealistic to be capable of building the perfect world which he envisaged.

Chamberlain's first visit to Bayreuth was in 1878 and his doctoral studies did not prevent his devoting much time to the Wagnerite cause of an "artwork of the future." After some unfortunate forays into financial speculation with a Frenchman named Cerceau which left him poorer, Chamberlain was forced to leave Geneva and, in 1885, settled in Dresden with his wife. From 1885 Chamberlain produced a large series of articles on Wagner and established himself as one of the leading exponents of Wagnerian art. His visits to Bayreuth brought him into personal contact with Cosima Wagner and the Wahnfried circle. His Wagnerian education included the study of Schopenhauer and Indian literature and philosophy as well Goethe and Kant, and it is a token of the depth of his immersion in these formative intellectual forces that, between 1905 and 1912, he published noteworthy studies of Kant, Indian philosophy and Goethe.

Chamberlain's political views in the Second Reich were

---

3 Although Chamberlain did not earn his doctorate since he did not wish to prepare for the comprehensive oral exam which was a requirement for the degree, he did publish his thesis in 1897 as *Recherches sur la sève ascendante* (Neuchâtel: Attinger).

4 The rise of plant sap was, interestingly, one of the proofs of the existence of an immaterial "Spirit of Nature" in the philosophical system of Henry More (1614-87), the Cambridge Neoplatonist; see More's *Enchiridium Metaphysicum* (1679), Ch.XXIV.

increasingly anti-Liberal and anti-Jewish. Even though Bismarck
turned away from his brief courting of the National Liberal party to
make a conservative alliance with agrarian and industrial interests,
Chamberlain agreed with Wagner's opinion that Bismarck too had
allowed himself to be entangled in electoral and factional politics.
With his growing sense of nationalism, so also grew Chamberlain's
anti-Semitism, a feature which he shared with Wagner. The Jews,
who had been emancipated in the Reich Constitution of 1871, were
popularly regarded by the Germans as morally inferior aliens, and
during the depression of 1873 they were widely portrayed as an
excessively powerful minority that had gained financial control over
the German host society and subverted the latter's cultural values. In
fact, Chamberlain developed this attitude so strongly that he even
criticized Kaiser Friedrich III for being too much of a "Jewish liberal"
diametrically opposed, as Chamberlain wrote to his aunt Harriet, to
what every intelligent and upright German felt. Germans were
everyday awakening more and more, he alleged, to the fact that "they
are menaced by complete moral and intellectual ruin if a strong
reaction does not set in against the supremacy of the Jews, who feed
upon them and suck out – at every grade of society – their very life
blood."[5]

Chamberlain's prolific writings as a publicist for Bayreuth in
the last years of the nineteenth century were devoted to the
establishment of Wagnerian art as the consummation of Aryan
cultural, social and political ideas, which could be sustained only
through anti-liberal, racial nationalism and a regenerated form of
Germanic Christianity.

In 1890 he made an important excursion to Bosnia, for, as he
recalled years later in a conversation with the Indologist Leopold von
Schroeder, it was Bosnia that first made him aware of the importance
of race.[6] He was struck by the purity and vitality of the Serbs as a race
and the superiority of their form of government, wherein an absolute
monarch led a free people. By contrast, he perceived the Austro-
Hungarian system of representative government as inefficiently
bureaucratic. In fact, Chamberlain was convinced that the Hapsburg
Empire was the inheritor of the decadence of the Roman Empire,
which had fallen as a result of racial miscegenation, and that the
contemporary decaying state of Austro-Hungary, which was selling

---

5 Letter dated June 26, 1886, quoted in G. Field, *op.cit.*, p.90.
6 G. Field, op.cit., p.98.

titles to Jews, was a proof of the deleterious power of philo-Semitism. His contempt for the Austrians increased his admiration of Bismarck's Prussia, since the latter at least demonstrated "in what simple ways it is possible not merely to theorize about race - but to breed and preserve it."[7]

In 1896, invited by Hugo Bruckmann, the Munich publisher, to write a survey of the cultural achievements of the nineteenth century, Chamberlain planned a three-part work of which the first was to review the cultural history of Europe from antiquity to 1800, the second to analyze the culture of the nineteenth century, and the third to outline the alternative of the ideals of the Wagnerian *Weltanschauung* to the growing tendency towards cultural degeneration. Only the first part of this enormous project was completed as *Die Grundlagen des neunzehnten Jahrhunderts* (München: F. Bruckmann, 1899). This work, like Count de Gobineau's *Essai sur l'inégalité des races humaines* (1853-55), was based on the primacy of race as the pivotal factor in the development and degeneration of nations. Chamberlain began with Greek art and philosophy, Roman law and organization, the revelation of Christ, and the racial chaos of the fall of the Roman Empire, and concluded with what he perceived as a conflict between the destructive commercialism of the Jews and the regenerative idealism of the Aryan race. The latter two sections are of significance particularly for the subsequent history of Germany, for in them he portrays Jews as predatory capitalists identified with mobile, unearned wealth, monopolies and international business syndicates. Liberal democracy and socialism were the political manifestations of the Jewish mentality which he declared "threatened to destroy our whole laboriously won civilization and culture."[8] The influence of the Jews was also held to be powerfully evident in the Roman Catholic Church which sought to rule the world on the basis of a Jewish materialistic tradition. By contrast, the Lutheran Reformation was evidence of the vital idealism of the German peoples, whereas the French Revolution was proof of the domination of the French people by Jewish and Jesuit influences.[9] Thus the *Grundlagen* was written, finally, as an attempt to identify and preserve the racial

---

7 *Rasse und Persönlichkeit,* München: F. Bruckmann, 1925, p.83,86.
8 See H.S. Chamberlain, *The Foundations of the Nineteenth Century*, tr. J. Lees, London: John Lane, 1911, p. 450.
9 Alfred Rosenberg in his *Die Spur des Juden im Wandel der Zeiten* (München, 1939), Ch.XII, presents the French Revolution as being secretly impelled by the anti-monarchic and predominantly Jewish-inspired cult of the Freemasons.

Gestalt of the Aryan peoples, for, "If we do not now resolve to investigate this problem resolutely and to cultivate race on principle, it will soon be too late and our Teutonic type will be lost forever."[10]

The *Grundlagen* was received with both adulation and sharp criticism, and among its staunchest defenders were not only German scholars and nationalists but Kaiser Wilhelm II himself. Wilhelm's anti-Semitism was in fact so strong that he confided to his son the Crown Prince in 1913 that Germany must "firmly exclude Jewish influence from the army and administration, and restrict its power in all artistic and literary activity."[11] Unfortunately, at the end of the first Great War, Wilhelm saw Germany's defeat, his own exile, and the establishment of the Weimar Republic as direct results of the pervasive conspiratorial power of the Jews. However, Chamberlain's writings crystallized the growing dissatisfaction among Germans with liberal politics, reckless urbanization, and materialistic science and technology, and encouraged the various agrarian, nationalist, racial and Germanic Christian movements that emerged at the turn of the century.

Chamberlain's personal life was marked by distress since his relationship with Anna gradually deteriorated until they were forced by ill health and ill temper to separate. But Chamberlain found a soul-mate in Wagner's daughter Eva, whom he decided to marry in December of 1908, following his divorce from Anna. Moving to Bayreuth, Chamberlain and Eva set up home in a house opposite Wagner's house, 'Wahnfried'. However, as international politics became steadily more menacing and Germany and England veered towards war, Chamberlain's distaste for Liberalism, commercialism and modernism grew and he decided to devote himself to attacking these forces politically and advancing what he regarded as the German idealist cause in politics as he had hitherto done in culture. Of the various tracts he wrote in this period, the most important is the *Politische Ideale*, though all his propaganda writings share the same themes, contrasting the conception of the German patriotic state with that of the party politics governing modern liberal democracies, between what Chamberlain perceived as real moral freedom versus the unruly selfishness of warring democratic parties, between the decaying Anglo-Saxon peoples and the still pure Teutonic. Already in 1902 Chamberlain had condemned the annexation of the Transvaal

---

10 Letter to Kaiser Wilhelm II in *Briefe*, II: 103.
11 Quoted in G. Field, *op.cit.*, p.254.

and Orange Free State just as he had approved Gladstone's earlier decision to concede independence to these Afrikaner republics. Chamberlain's correspondence with Cosima Wagner at this time reveals his close identification of the Boer War with Jewish financial and mine-owning interests, and his contempt for the new materialistic England was as great as his admiration and yearning for the older aristocratic one of the mid-Victorian age. As he told Cosima Wagner, "This is the result when one has studied politics with a Jew [Disraeli] for a quarter of a century."[12]

Fully convinced of the eventual decline of the British Empire and of the degeneracy of France and Russia, Chamberlain firmly concluded that "the future of mankind depends on a powerful Germany extending far across the earth."[13] However, the contest between Germany and Britain and France was actually initiated by England and France, whom Chamberlain declared had decided to destroy Germany as a rising world-force, attributing this decision to the fact that these two countries had fallen into the hands of the Jews. A person could not explain World War I he argued, except in terms of the *Judentum* and the commercial control of the world - a war against *Bildung,* moral strength, non-commercial art and every idealist perspective on life, for the benefit of a world that would honor only industry, finance, and trade - in short, unrestricted plutocracy.[14]

Chamberlain's war tracts were extremely popular in Germany, and his *Politische Ideale* sold 34,000 copies in just over a month after it was published. In all, as Field reports, "it is probable that somewhere between 750,000 and a million copies of his essays were bought during the course of the war."[15] To the Germans the war was one that was waged to save civilization.

From 1916 onwards Chamberlain began to suffer from a form of Parkinson's disease so that he increasingly lost the use his limbs and could only barely speak. But he continued to produce books and letters including the autobiographical *Lebenswege meines Denkens* (1919), *Mensch und Gott* (1921), and *Rasse und Persönlichkeit* (1925). Reflecting on the lost war, Chamberlain concluded that the German army had been betrayed by the press and politicians,

---

12 Chamberlain to Cosima Wagner, Sept.16,1900, *Briefwechsel zwischen Cosima Wagner und Fürst Ernst zu Hohenlohe-Langenburg,* Stuttgart, 1937, p.605.
13 *Briefe,* II:138.
14 Letter of January 20, 1917, to Kaiser Wilhelm, *Briefe,* II: 252.
15 G. Field, op.cit., p.390.

especially Bethmann-Hollweg whom he referred to as a "Frankfurter pimp,"[16] alluding to the Chancellor's merchant and banker ancestors. He noted with alarm the success of "Jewish culture" at the end of the war, and his disgust with the new state of affairs was echoed around Germany in the growing number of anti-Jewish associations. Chamberlain's impatience with the Weimar Republic was alleviated only by the hope that a new Germany might arise from the ashes of the Second Reich. This rebirth was in fact initiated by the National Socialist movement which, by 1923, had become a radical nationalist force under the leadership of Hitler. Chamberlain met Hitler in September when the latter visited Bayreuth and was immediately convinced of the latter's destiny as the German leader who would restore the true culture of Germany, including the Wagnerian ideal to which Hitler subscribed as strongly as did Chamberlain himself. In his letter of October 7,1923, to Hitler, Chamberlain enthusiastically counselled Hitler that

> the German's organizational skills are unsurpassed... and his scientific capacity is unequalled - in the essay *Politische Ideale* I pinned my hope on this. The ideal kind of politics is to have none. But this non-politics must be frankly acknowledged and forced upon the world through the exercice of power.[17]

Earlier in the same letter he stated that part of the reason of his admiration of Hitler was that he perceived Hitler as

> the opposite of a politician ... for the essence of all politics is membership of a party, whereas with you all parties disappear, consumed by the heat of your love for the fatherland.

In a later writing he endorsed Hitler's anti-Semitic views, stating that:

> [Hitler] recognizes and proclaims that one cannot simultaneously embrace Jesus and those who crucified

---

16 Letter dated Dec. 24,1914, to Max von Baden, quoted in G. Field, *op.cit.,* p.382.
17 *Briefe*, II:124ff.

him. That is the splendid thing about Hitler – his courage! In this respect he reminds one of Luther.[18]

In fact the entire Wahnfried circle was enthusiastic about Hitler, and Siegfried Wagner and his English wife Winifred were active supporters of his cause. However, it is apparent that none of them, including Chamberlain, would have condoned any of the violence that came to be associated with the name of Hitler.[19] Even Alfred Rosenberg, Chamberlain's most significant Nazi Party ideological disciple, never proposed the extermination of what he perceived to be the Jewish enemy but only their exclusion from all political and intellectual affairs of the state.[20] In fact, Chamberlain's *Politische Ideate* was not conceived as a political treatise so much as a sketch of the dangers of the divisive impact of party politics on the unity of a society. National unity was a newly won achievement for the German peoples, who had suffered from centuries or even millennia of internecine war and now had the chance to work together and to think and act politically as a unified nation. This was an ideal that was ensconced deeply in the Germanic psyche of his time. What made Chamberlain's *Politische Ideale* so momentously significant was both its timing and Chamberlain's close contacts with the rulers of Germany prior to both world wars.

---

18 "Adolf Hitler", *Deutsche Presse* (München), April 20-21, 1924, p.1.

19 Eva Chamberlain is reported to have expressly declared, after the Reichskristallnacht, that "My husband would not have liked this!" (quoted in G. Field, *op.cit.,* p.12).

20 A. Rosenberg, *Die Spur des Juden im Wandel der Zeiten,* München, 1939, p.152f.: "It must be determined national-politically that 1) The Jews are recognized as a 'nation' living in Germany ... 3) The Jews do not have the right to engage in German politics in speech, writing, or deed. 4) The Jews do not have the right to hold state offices and to serve in the army either as soldiers or as officers.... 5) The Jews do not have the right to be leaders in state and communal cultural institutions (theaters, galleries, etc.) and to hold positions as professors and teachers in Germany schools and universities. ... 6) The Jews do not have the right to represent the German Reich in economic agreements; they also do not have the right to be represented in the directory of state banks and of communal credit institutions ... 8) Zionism must be energetically supported in order that a certain number of German Jews may be yearly ordered to Palestine or, generally, out of our borders."

II: The Prussian antecedents of Chamberlain's politics: Paul de Lagarde and Heinrich von Treitschke

Although the intellectual antecedents of Chamberlain's work are varied and include Kant, Herder, Goethe, and Wagner, the chief forerunners of Chamberlain's political ideas are the Prussians, Paul de Lagarde (1827-91) and Heinrich von Treitschke (1834-96).[21] Like Chamberlain, Lagarde was both a religious and a political thinker.[22] In his collection of essays, *Deutsche Schriften* (Göttingen, 1886), Lagarde outlined his conception of the ideal Prussian conservative state with the same denunciations of the liberal and democratic ethic that are to be found in Chamberlain. In 'Über das Verhältnis des deutschen Staates zu Theologie, Kirche und Religion', for example, Lagarde points to the German - that is, Kantian and Fichtean -notion

---

21 Constantin Frantz (1817-1891) is to some extent similar to Lagarde, though his distinctive contribution to German politics is his concept of federalism which involved the leadership of a union of German states by Prussia and Austria together (see A. Jacob, *Europa: German Conservative Foreign Policy 1870-1940,* Lanham, MD: University Press of America, 2001, Ch.II; cf. "The political thought of Constantin Frantz", in *The Third Reich,* International Council for Philosophy and Humanistic Studies, London: Weidenfeld and Nicolson, 1955,112-147).

22 Paul de Lagarde was the adopted name of Paul Bötticher, professor of oriental languages at the University of Göttingen, theologian and conservative political thinker. For a comprehensive study of Lagarde's thought, see Jean Favrel, *La pensée de Paul de Lagarde (1827-1891)*, Paris: Librairie Honorie Champion, 1979.

def - freedom means to be what God intended you to be!

of freedom which is truly philosophical, unlike the empty French slogans of 'liberté' and 'egalité'. As he says, "He is not free who "can do what he will, but who can become what he should,"[23] and, again, liberty is defined as "the right to become what God granted us to become." As a corollary of the philosophical notion of freedom, equality is considered a defect, since inequality alone can build a true harmony of relationships between the different individuals which constitute a state.[24] In fact, the absurdity of the French Revolution was that the nation was split into an atomic constitution of individuals and ceased to be an organism.[25]

Lagarde's conservatism supported the racial and ethical value of the aristocracy. However, he was disappointed that the Prussian princes had shown themselves more egoistic and self-indulgent than politically visionary leaders. Applauding Stein's plans for *Selbstverwaltung* or autonomous administration, Lagarde desires the completion of Stein's projects which were unfortunately left unfinished. As regards the masses, Lagarde is convinced of the lack of discernment among the people as such, that is, as individuals, for

> The people do not at all speak when the single individuals of whom the people consist speak. The people speak only when the nationality in the individuals is expressed.[26]

Like Chamberlain, Lagarde insists also on technical competence on the part of those making decisions on public life and on the participation of all of the qualified members of the public in such matters:

> I would have the government be controlled only through those who have already learned to judge and to direct public life in smaller circles, before they begin to judge and direct the public life at a higher level: it is a question, in my opinion, above all, of technical competence, and insofar as this knowledge is present in people who are not government officials, the people should also exercise a control of the government; but those who do not have this technique

---

23 *Deutsche Schriften*, p.85 (my translations).

24 cf. 'Programm für die konservative Partel Preussens', *op.cit.*, p.466.

25 'Über das Verhältnis', *op.cit*, p.45.

26 'Über die gegenwärtige Lage des deutschen Reichs', *op.cit.*, p.152.

should neither abrogate the right of expressing their opinion, nor should the affairs of the life of the state placed by the nature of things in secret and under the sole appreciation of competent persons be subjected to the judgements of the uninitiated.[27]

In general, the people's participation in the affairs of the state is only supplementary to the supreme commandership of the monarch who represents in his person the highest law and duty of the land.[28]

Naturally, in such a conception of a monarchic state with the people recruited occasionally according to their talent to direct specific local and national policies, there is no place for a parliament, though the Kaiser would be aided in the administration by a chancellor and ministers and provincial prefects. The leadership of the nation would remain with the princes by virtue of their noble lineage and they would ensure the consolidation of the monarchy by their natural support of the Kaiser.[29] Lagarde thus sought to preserve as far as possible a feudal government in the Prussia of Bismarck. However, given the imperfect virtue of the present nobility, Lagarde allows that in certain cases it might be better to have an elite of talent take the place of the princes, for the monarchy would be equally supported by it. The role of the aristocracy or the elite of the nation would be that of mediator between the king and the people, and, exactly as Chamberlain characterizes them, Lagarde describes the latter as the "matter" to be animated by the aristocracy, who represent indeed the genuine "Volk."[30] At the same time, the people represent the limit of the activity of the aristocracy, so that the relation between the masses and the elite would be a thoroughly organic one. Like Chamberlain, Lagarde too envisages a certain political role for the middle classes, but only when they have demonstrated a sufficient degree of self-awareness and governmental aptitude.[31]

As for the modern system of parliamentary representation, Lagarde, like Chamberlain, sees it as "a great falsehood"[32] since the election of deputies to the Reichstag on direct and universal suffrage

---

27 'Die nächsten Pflichten deutscher Politik', *op.cit.*, p. 531.

28 'Programm', *op.cit;* p.456.

29 *Ibid.*, p.463.

30 'Konservativ?', *op.cit.*,p.11.

31 cf. 'Die Religion der Zukunft', *op.cit.*, p.316.

32 'Über die gegenwärtige Lage des deutschen Reichs', *op.cit.*, p.152.

means the subjection of government to voters who lack discernment and are foolishly swayed by the machinations of political parties. It is necessary therefore to suppress the system of political parties as well as the various legislative assemblies.[33] The Prussian government already corresponded in many respects to Lagarde's ideal since, in 1817, Friedrich Wilhelm IV had instituted a Staatsrat named by the Kaiser and not subject to the Reichstag, and a similar body was sought to be reestablished in 1884 by Bismarck. In 1881, Bismarck had also set up a Volkswirtschaftsrat in Prussia composed of experts named by the government and the chambers of commerce which would decide questions of economic legislation, regardless of the Reichstag.[34]

Lagarde's idea of deputing the control of the budget and the elaboration of legislative texts no longer to the Reichstag but to permanent Stände, or representative corporatist orders, to be assisted by the Staatsrat, is exactly followed by Chamberlain in his *Politische Ideate*. The Reichstag, which would thereby be rendered virtually impotent, would be called upon only occasionally to act as a 'Schiedsgericht' or a tribunal for arbitration in cases of dispute between the members of the Stände and the government. The Stände envisaged by Lagarde would be constituted of delegates of the provincial states, of the chambers of commerce and of the principal noble families. Not elected at all, they would not be an artificial political fabrication, but an organic political formation.[35] In every case requiring deliberation, only those members would officiate who are suited for the task at hand and not all, as in the case of a parliament, where the diversity of the members tends to mutually neutralize all important questions. Finally, even given the deliberations of the Stände, their decisions are tantamount to advisory recommendations to the king who will have the ultimate word in making a decision, for he is supreme as both legislative and executive power. Not surprisingly, Lagarde's plan of the establishment of a

---

33 "'Die nächsten Pflichten', *op.cit.*, p.518.

34 Bismarck's efforts to extend this council to the entire nation in the form of a National Economic Council were however defeated by the Reichstag, in June 1881. For an interesting discussion of Bismarck's experiments in corporatist government, see R.H. Bowen, *German theories of the corporative state with special reference to the period 1870-1919*, N.Y.: McGraw-Hill Co., 1947, pp. 148-156.

35 Lagarde, 'Die nächsten Pflichten', *op.cit.*, p.531f.

State High Court is only for the purpose of investigating complaints against the administrative organs, including the chancellory and the ministry, but not against the organs of decision, the king and his direct representatives, for the latter are above the law as the very embodiment of the political ethos.

Lagarde's quasi-feudal state is a defense of the monarchical ideal against the parliament which "engulfs like a parasitical plant the power of the crown and degrades the king to the point of making him the first functionary of the state machine."[36] He perceives capital as another dangerous threat to the monarchy. As he explains,

> The stock exchange is a curse for the people since it renders possible ... the acquisition of a fortune of unheard of abundance which totally escapes the obligation of serving either others or the possessor: a proprietor of land needs, the more widespread his lands are, a greater number of men to render it valuable; the man of money may content himself with accumulating the interest from his capital without giving the least part of it to anyone except to his money agent.[37]

Landed property is perceived by Lagarde as a healthy and altruistic source of economy as opposed to the exploitative industrial and bank economy. The fact that a large number of financiers were Jewish was one of the many reasons why he was opposed to the Semites living in Germany, whom he perceived as an alien and destructive "nation within a nation," characterized by capitalistic and liberalist features but spiritually sterile, possessing in his opinion no truly religious or artistic capacity. Lagarde's solution was the abjuration, either self-willed or forced, of the Jewish tradition by its members so that they would be absorbed into Christian German society. Such a proposal was at best unrealistic since, as he himself noted, the Jewish 'nation' was sufficiently strong to be able to reassert itself even after a century of mixed marriages.[38]

* * *

---

36 'Programm', op.cit., p.428.
37 Schriften für das deutsche Volk (München: J.F. Lehmann, 1934), Vol.11, Sec.V, 'Judentum', p.240.
38 'Zum Unterrichtsgezetze', op.cit., p.237.

A more vigorously militaristic idea of the state is presented in the writings of Heinrich von Treitschke. Unlike Hegel, Treitschke took care to distinguish the state from the nation. The state is not an organic growth, but rather one that must be guided by historical reason, or that reason based on the experience of historical events. Treitschke disagreed in particular with Hegel's view that the state is the fullest realization of the moral Idea and representative of "the whole of a nations's life."[39] Rather, Treitschke believed that the state is an external construct of the nation: "The state ... is only the people as a force" and "the framework of all national life." A nationalistic state supported by *military force* would thus be an indomitably powerful institution.

Treitschke believed that, if the nationalistic condition were fulfilled, Machiavelli was indeed right in his claim that "The State is power." However, in insisting that the individual must submit his will to that of the state, Treitschke reveals a close resemblance also to the conservatism of Burke and Carlyle:

> The greatness of the State lies precisely in its power of uniting the past with the present and the future; and consequently no individual has the right to regard the State as the servant of his own aims but is bound by moral duty and the physical necessity to subordinate himself to it, while the State lies under the obligation to concern itself with the life of its citizens by extending to them its help and protection.[40]

While individuals must submit their will to that of the State, the State will submit *its* will to no other power, except at the risk of losing its existence altogether. The State thus becomes a kind of substitute for God: "The Christian duty of self-sacrifice for something higher has no existence whatever for the State, because there is nothing whatever beyond it in world-history."[41]

Like Fichte and Mazzini, Treitschke deplored all forms of materialism and insisted that the state "is a moral community called to

39 Heinrich von Treitschke, *Politics,* tr. A.J. Balfour, N.Y. The Macmillan Co., 1916, I, p.53.
40 *Ibid.,* p.61.
41 *Selections from Treitschke's Lectures on Politics*, tr. A.L. Gowans, London: Gowans and Gray Ltd., 1914, 32.

positive labor for the improvement of the human race, and its ultimate aim is to build up real national character through and within itself, for this is the highest moral duty of nations as well as of individuals."[42] Treitschke maintained that the state must be uniform in its spiritual complexion since

> The consciousness of national unity is dependent upon a common bond of religion, for religious sentiment is one of the fundamental forces of the human character. Jewish pretensions first tampered with this truth by interchanging the conceptions of religion and ritual. Ritual differences may indeed be endured by a great nation, although with difficulty... but the coexistence of several religions within one nationality, involving an irreconcilable and ultimately intolerable difference of outlook upon, life, can only be a transitional phenomenon.[43]

Treitschke indeed modifies the Kantian and Fichtean doctrine of the Moral law so that it is made to be, not the basis of a universal political order, but the model on which all nations evolve their own independent cultures. As H.W.C. Davis puts it, according to Treitschke, "There is no such thing as a universal moral law or an ideally best constitution. These conceptions are founded on the doctrine that all States and all human beings must conform to the Law of Nature (Naturrechtslehre)."[44]

Democracy, with its notion of universal suffrage, is perceived as absurd since

> it remains a sound principle to exclude the wholly irresponsible section of society from the exercise of a right which implies a capacity for independent judgment. [The effective right to vote] is more a duty of citizenship than an individual prerogative, and since it must be exercised for the common good, i.e. for the good of the State, it must rest with the State to decide who shall exercise it. This right becomes unreasonable when pushed to its furthest conclusion, and ignores the time-

---

42 *Politics*, I:74.

43 *Politics,* I: 334.

44 H.W.C. Davis, *The Political Thought of Heinrich von Treitschke,* N.Y.: C. Scribner's Sons, 1915, p.124; cf. Treitschke, *Politics,* I, 326-8.

honored truth long ago laid down by Aristotle, that the
greatest wrong is to equalize the unequal.[45]

The result of universal suffrage would be that "a
disproportionate share of influence is given to stupidity, superstition,
malice and mendacity, crude egoism, and nebulous waves of
sentiment, all of which introduce an incalculable element into the life
of the State."[46] Democracy will deliver the people to the bluster and
violence of political parties:

> The strongest lungs always prevail with the mob, and
> there is now no hope of eliminating that peculiar truth
> of brutality and that coarsening and vulgarizing element
> which has entered into public life. These consequences
> are unavoidable, and unfortunately react upon the
> whole moral outlook of the people; just as the
> unchecked railing and lying of the platform corrupts the
> tone of daily intercourse. Beyond this comes the further
> danger that the really educated classes withdraw more
> and more from a political struggle which adopts such
> methods.[47]

Intellectual life will generally suffer since "industrial and financial
talents do indeed take root and flourish, but... the subtler and deeper
qualities find no natural soil, nor indeed can they ever, for the natures
which possess them are aristocrats born."[48]

Treitschke's political philosophy is indeed one of the most
aristocratic, representing as it does the mind of the Prussian ruling
class of his time. The fact of classes within a society can never be
eradicated since inequality will always exist between people: "Just as
the State cannot survive unless divided into rulers on the one hand
and subjection on the other, neither can society unless organized into
various classes."[49] The masses will ever remain the masses, and the
lower classes are indeed necessary for the flourishing of culture, since,
"in every well-ordered community, there must be an undermost layer
which contains everything that cannot maintain itself on a higher

---

45 *Ibid.*, II:196.
46 *Ibid.*
47 *Ibid.*, II:198.
48 *Ibid.*, II:294.
49 *Ibid.*, I:322.

level - and yet from this same class springs the rejuvenating and reviving force of every nation."[50] The lower classes have their own joys and are not to be pitied or despised on account of their poverty, as the materialistic, and rationalistic movements of the age proclaim them to be. The duty of the State is only to keep the poverty of these classes within limits and to make it endurable:

> Long ago Aristotle defined the position of this class within the state in words essentially true, though tinged with the hard-heartedness of antiquity. 'They are content', he said, 'when they are permitted to busy themselves with their own affairs'.[51]

Unlike Hegel, who favored a constitutional monarchy, Treitschke insisted on a monarchy that was supreme not only in name, but also in power. "The minimum test of monarchy is whether or not the will of the monarch can be overruled ... It is an ancient experience that monarchy presents more perfectly than any other form of government a tangible expression of political power and national unity."[52] Treitschke did support a parliamentary system constituted of two houses, an upper and a lower, but the role of this parliament was not one of active interference in the monarchical rule of the nation, but rather of a catalystic review of the activities of the monarchy. It could not, by any means, bring about the fall of ministers, even though it may criticize them. The real power of the monarch in Treitschke's system is a contrast to the relative impotence of the constitutional monarchy in nineteenth century Britain which had lost the glory it possessed in the Tudor age.

A monarchy will obviate what is indeed the real danger of a democracy, and that is that it becomes "a complete plutocracy, an oligarchy of a few big banking houses, who avail themselves of democratic forms, in order to exploit them for their own ends."[53] Monarchy, on the other hand, is "based on the idea that it is the conscious will of individuals which makes history, and not the mysterious brainless power of public opinion." The existence of a monarchy is, in the last analysis, necessary since it puts the highest positions of authority out of reach of adventurers and parties. Indeed, monarchy is the form of government most suited to the fostering of

---

50 *Ibid.*
51 *Ibid.*, II:323.
52 *Ibid.*, II:59.
53 *Ibid.*, II:275.

individual liberty which is the prime rational virtue of civilized man, for it is most suited to exhibiting and maintaining the authority of the laws which is an "indispensable condition of liberty." In this definition of liberty as being "based upon reasonable laws and their observance," Treitschke reveals his affinity with the firm idealistic tradition of Fichte, Kant and Carlyle. Treitschke also favored the continuance of the aristocracy as a support for the monarch, although this admiration of the aristocracy may have been partly based on his concern to preserve the Prussian Junkers in power.

Treitschke's staunch nationalism was, not surprisingly, combined with racialistic views as well. All nations were not, according to him, equal, and Germany was indeed the highest of all European nations. The English were a shallow people, while their American relatives were marked by "an energetic materialism on economic lines combined with an indifference to the intangible possessions of intellectual life.'[54] The Russians, too, were little more than barbarians posing as civilized peoples. As for the Mongol races, they were incapable of truly aristocratic conduct, while the Negroid races were naturally destined to slavery. He was naturally anti-Semitic, and considered the Jews to be an insidious element in society:

> a dangerous disintegrating force lurked in this people who were able to assume the mask of any other nationality. Fair-minded Jews must themselves admit that after a nation has become conscious of its own personality, there is no place left for the cosmopolitanism of the Semites.[55]

The only means of counteracting the pernicious influence of the Jews on the state was

> to arouse an energy of national pride, so real that it becomes a second nature to repel involuntarily everything which is foreign to the Germanic nature. This principle must be carried into everything; it must apply to our visits to the theater and to the music-hall as much as to the reading of the newspapers. Whenever he finds his life sullied by the filth of Judaism, the German must turn from it, and learn to speak the truth boldly about

---

54 *Ibid.*, II:317.
55 *Ibid.*, I:300f.

it.[56]

According to Treitschke, national political traditions represent the "objectively revealed will of God." [57] The nationalistic state supported by military force was the main goal of his political philosophy. An army well prepared for war was, according to Treitschke, one of the prime virtues of a State, since it fosters patriotism, national unity, and personal character. War too is glorified in the following manner: "The grandeur of war lies in the utter annihilation of puny man in the great conception of the State, and it brings out the full magnificence of the sacrifice of fellow-countrymen for one another."[58]

56 *Ibid.*, I:301f.
57 *Ibid.*, I:13
58 *Ibid.* II:66f.

greatest wrong is
to equalize the
unequal —
ARISTOTLE

III : The "ideal state" of Houston Stewart Chamberlain

The political doctrines of Lagarde and Treitschke are repeated in several points by Chamberlain in his *Politische Ideale*. The initial premise of Chamberlain's political ideal is that the state is an organism just as human beings are and is therefore to be organized naturally, or scientifically, rather than artificially as it has hitherto been. In this view of state processes, Chamberlain is very much a follower of Herder's organismic theory of the nation which is based on the primacy of language and race.[59] In his understanding of the supra-national operations of Nature, Chamberlain also reflects the political notions of philosophers of the Unconscious like Eduard von Hartmann (1842-1906) and C.G. Jung (1875-1961).[60] The advantage of Chamberlain's view is that it considers the state to be created not by man "as freedom," who is ruled by his self-will, but by man "as nature," that is, as participating in the higher unconscious operations of Nature as Providence. It is the same Nature as Providence which initiated the earliest state formations by the invention of agriculture among the original hunting populations, for the invention of agriculture freed those henceforth devoted to it from the need of roving over

---

59 For an interesting study of Herder's political philosophy, see P.M. Barnard, *Herder's social and political thought: From Enlightenment to Nationalism,* Oxford: Clarendon Press, 1965; cf. also F.W. Coker, *Organismic theories of the State,* N.Y.: Columbia Univ. Press, 1910.

60 See W. Odajnyk, *Jung and Politics: The political and social ideas of C.G. Jung,* N.Y.: Harper and Row, 1976, and Alexander Jacob, *De Naturae Natura: A study of idealistic conceptions of Nature and the Unconscious,* Stuttgart: F. Steiner, 1992.

distant lands in search of food and allowed them to settle in a
restricted area which they could gradually develop into a state. The
natural formation and development of the state by Nature is
inexorable and inevitable, in spite of the temporary obstructions and
delays which are imposed on it by the accidents of temporal history.
The only significant, and hence really 'historic,' events are not battle-
and coronation-dates, but those which mark the turn of an age in the
story of mankind through the adoption of revolutionary new ideas
regarding man's social or cultural life. These revolutions are effected
by "deeply religious enthusiastic natures" inspired by the power of
Nature. Such cultural geniuses are men in tune with the entire racial
consciousness (or the Unconscious) of their group and only a politics
that is geared to this same racial Unconscious can succeed in a
significant way.

Of all the major nations at the turn of the century only
Germany is capable of doing this, since "Germany alone ... is capable
of grasping this thought in a new orientation of human politics that
follows a higher reason" (p.66). The other nations are all, to a greater
or lesser degree, under the stultifying influence of the paltry
rationalistic ideas of the French Revolution, and Germany alone is
capable of resisting the fascinations of this false ideal.[61] Thus only
Germany is providentially suited for the leadership of the world: "The
future of mankind depends on whether Germany is equal to this
expectation - let us calmly say this destiny - or not." (p.67)

The first step to a reorganization of the state is to clearly
recognize and reject the French ideals, which are based on the
infamous slogan of "liberty, equality, fraternity." Chamberlain
exposes each of these ideas as a lie since the so-called 'liberty' of the
French Revolution does not exist among man as nature, who is born
not free but extremely dependent on the protection of his family. The
real freedom of man is not something that he is born with but
something which he must strive for throughout his life as the
realization of his moral nature.[62] The equality of men is equally

---

61 In his abhorrence of the French political notions Chamberlain is a descendant
of Ernst Moritz Arndt (1769-1860), whose nationalistic writings are also
motivated by a love of the Teutonic race and language and a contempt of the
French. See A.G. Pundt, *Arndt and the nationalist awakening of Germany,* N.Y.:
Columbia Press, 1935.
62 Chamberlain's politics, in basing itself on the Kantian doctrine of the moral
law, resembles in many ways the political philosophy of J.G. Fichte (1762-1814).

delusory since, quite obviously, neither in physical nor in moral virtue is any man really the equal of another. As for the political cry of "fraternity," this is an empty noise that ignores the fact that "not love but duty lies under the conception of the state." (p.73) In short, the French slogan is typical of "Gallic insolence, nothing more; insolence born of shallow thought, united with aimless desire." Indeed, history has shown that the French revolutionary ideals have introduced only anarchy and despotism instead of freedom, irreverence instead of equality, and hatred instead of brotherhood. From this triumvirate of disobedience, irreverence, and hate arise "tyranny, mediocrity, heartlessness," or "despotic government, oppression of the significant, deadening of the public body to iniquity and, generally, to injustice and suffering." (p.75)

The infiltration of the French revolutionary ideals into English politics is evident in the gradual transformation of the older aristo-cratic traditions - especially under the influence of the Jewish Prime Minister, Benjamin Disraeli (1804-1881) - to increasingly revolutionary modes of operation, until finally the office of the Prime Minister has become as powerful as that of an absolute king. Fortunately, the English people themselves are one of the most conservative in the world, and so the parliamentary movement has not altered their sensibility thoroughly yet. Even within Germany, the Social Democrat party has succumbed to the French Revolutionary ideals. But the German workers must soon realize that these notions are foreign to their spirit and inimical to them.

In marked contrast, the new Germanic revolution will be based on a uniform morality of obedience, subordination and duty. Germany is, compared to the comfort-loving American and the artful Japanese, a young and vigorous nation and it has the advantage of being scientifically more disciplined than the other nations. Just as in the realm of natural science, so too in politics, Germany will be organized vitally in accordance with divine Nature. The anthropomorphism of Rousseau's conception of the state as a social contract takes no cognizance of the fact that states arise naturally among men as much as among ants (this also repudiates the absurd theories of the

---

For Fichte's conception of liberty as well as of his monarchic ideal, see his *Grundlage des Naturrechts nach Principien der Wissenschaftslehre,* in *Sämtliche Werke,* III. For his tentative notions of a corporate state, see his *Der geschlossene Handelsstaat,loc.cit.,* while his nationalistic ideals are best displayed in his *Reden an die deutsche Nation.*

anarchists that man should live without a government). Like Kant and
Fichte, Chamberlain envisages the state as the arena in which man
realizes his humanity, and the individual may not demand benefits
from the state so much as the latter demand duties from the former.
Just as Nature does not regard the individual in the larger design of
the preservation of species, so too the state does not concern itself
with the individual so much as with the humanity in him.[63]

One of the prime conditions for the successful realization of
man as a political entity is the permanence of the state. It is this
duration which allows the individual to look beyond the span of his
own lifetime to the future generations that he will endow with his
work and ideas. Therein, too, lies the value of hereditary property,
which is Nature's way of ensuring the duration of a man's labor and of
his love for his family long after his death. How different is
Proudhon's characterization of property as "robbery"! The collective
possessions of the Communistic state are a more primitive form of
economics for individual possession spurs men into endeavors whose
effects reach beyond their individual lives and, indeed, beyond their
immediate families into the culture of the whole state, which is both
the condition and the true end of these endeavors. It must be noted too
that by 'possession' Chamberlain means above all immobile
possession, that is, landed property, since the soil alone is intimately
linked to the formation and growth of a state. Opposed to this true
foundation of the state is the modern money economy which
encourages a restlessness among its possessors and a tendency
towards change and catastrophes of every sort. The remedy to this
modern malaise, suggests Chamberlain, is perhaps to confiscate all
the private financial institutions and to nationalize them. This will
obviate the accumulation of billions and private monopolies without
any real work. The danger of capitalism is that it gives free rein to the
self-will of the moneyed man which discounts the personal freedom
of others to such an extent that it has, in America, virtually enslaved
six year old children in its factories (p.90). Although Chamberlain
does not specifically characterize the financier as a Jew, it is evident
from his later writings and from his *Grundlagen* that he saw the

---

63 For a similar view of the state as the collective embodiment of the humanity of
the individuals constituting it, see E.M. Arndt, *Geist derZeit,* I, in *Werke,* VI,
p.107, and III, in *Werke,* VIII, p.108. Arndt's politics, constituted of monarchic,
aristocratic, corporatist, and nationalistic elements, are indeed very similar to
Fichte's as well as to Lagarde's and Chamberlain's (see, Pundt, *op.cit.).*

Jewish capitalist as the prime enemy of the Germanic nationalistic ideal. This is made clear in his letter to a friend which declared that, in spite of his avoidance of explicit references to the Jews, the anti-Jewish spirit of his *Politische Ideale* would be immediately understood by the Germans.[64]

Chamberlain then considers the constitutional question and straightway notes the inadequacy of popular representation. Popular rule could work only in a very small state, as Aristotle had declared[65] and even in ancient Athens all the greatness of the Greek state was accomplished under the rule of autocrats, while the degeneration of it was due entirely to the populace, "who were called, out of well-minded foolish idealism, to cooperation and decision in questions for which they possessed no aptitude nor ever will" (p.91). Parliamentarism is prone to all manner of weaknesses such as demagogy, electoral manipulation, and a complete lack of political discernment among inefficient members of parliament. Chamberlain reminds his reader of Goethe's dictum that "Nothing is more repulsive than the majority" (p.93). For even a dictatorship is more admirable than the foolish rule of the populace in that it calls forth unusual strength of character. In Germany, fortunately the Council of Ministers and the Chancellor of the Reich have constantly stemmed the rise of the rule of the majority, just as in England too the older aristocratic tradition has persisted in spite of the growing influence of parliamentarism in the country. In criticizing the French political system, Chamberlain adduces the authority of the sociologist Gustave le Bon (1841-1931) who had studied the absurdly contradictory results of mass psychology during the French Revolution.[66]

As for the socialist ideal which has arisen as an off-shoot from the French revolutionary ethos, this too is completely alien to the German people, whose vigorous social activity must be rechannelled from the allurements of foreign socialist propaganda into the native fidelity to the soil and to God, who is the Intellectual principle of all natural phenomena. The falseness of the socialist ideal is exposed by the fact that contrary to its "progressive" pretensions, it is indeed a reactionary movement which sets man back to prehistoric times, and

---

64 See G. Field, *Evangelist of Race: The Germanic Vision of Houston Stewart Chamberlain*, N.Y.: Columbia Univ. Press, p.378.

65 Aristotle, *Ethica Nichomachea*, 1170b31.

66 In his important work, *La Révolution française et la psychologie des révolutions*, Paris: E. Flammarion, 1912.

no amount of allusion to the ancient democracies of Athens and Rome
will vindicate the communists when the Athenian politics was based
on a slave-economy and the Roman on the firm foundation of the
family unit. He perceives the horrible results of socialist doctrine in
what he calls the anarchy in plutocratic America, Italy, and France
(p.102).

The opposite of the benighted communistic notions of the state
is the monarchical idea, which represents the highest development of
a state since, in the monarch, the people have learnt to symbolize all
of their highest aspirations and ideals. The monarch is the most
unselfish member of the nation since he is the embodiment of
political duty and of the natural subordination of all people according
to merit within the body politic for the general welfare of the whole.
The insolence of the revolutionary youth in a revolutionary state is
substituted with the reverential attitude of the truly cultured human
being. At the same time, a monarchy must be supported by scientific
organization of the state, by which Chamberlain means the
"adaptation of the means to the goal to be achieved" (p.105), that is,
the "division of labor" according to the talent of the individual, and
the awareness of the interconnection of all parts of the state to one
another, instead of the deplorable social 'atomism' of the democratic
systems.

In this context, Chamberlain points particularly to the apparent
success of England as a colonial power. England has ruled the world
through a strength of character which has encouraged the rapacity of
individuals and a concomitant brutality of method, but it has at the
same time neglected the development of intellectual, and especially
philosophical, culture. The spread of English values throughout the
world is therefore a great danger since it means the propagation of
social atomism and crass utilitarianism. The weapon with which
Germany may defeat this weak empire is that of scientific political
organization and spiritual concentration, for, as he says, "To the true
organic subordination of the individual - the polar opposite of slavery
- belongs a higher culture than the English system demands or even
just allows" (p.112). As the American Admiral, Alfred Thayer Mahan
(1840-1914) had remarked, organicism of state-formation is most
evident in the Prussian state, for "it lets itself be plastically modelled
by a strong government, without the individual forfeiting the power of
initiative in the circle of activity peculiar to him" (p.114).[67] We note

---

67 A.T. Mahan, *The Influence of Sea-Power upon History*, Boston: Little, Brown,

once again in the Germanic political ideal the role of a strong government and the salutary limitation of an individual's activity to the social circle best suited to his natural talents.

Germany's multiplicity of principalities is a boon to the nation since "multiplicity belongs precisely to organic life"[68] and is a sign of its higher development. The monarchy is only strengthened by the numerous princes of his kingdom since they all reflect, in their own peculiar regional ways, their devotion to the monarchical ideal, and preclude the disastrous sameness of the egalitarian democratic doctrine.[69] As opposed to the external changes sought by the socialists, Chamberlain points to the internal freedom insisted on by Kant, who was indeed the greatest revolutionary of modern times. True freedom is the inner self-realization of man as man, and every man is required to prepare himself in his society for this basic human task.[70] Only then will every citizen be possessed of his innate dignity as a member of an enlightened nation, and only then will every individual cease to be a means to a political end but a goal unto himself. The lack of this individual goal is the lack of true freedom and the harshest slavery that one could be subjected to. Gainsaying the Nietzschean glorification of the will to power as a crude philosophical egotism, Chamberlain stresses the regeneration of Germany, and through the Germans the rest of mankind, through politics based on the strict moral law of Kant and on the disciplined scientific organization of society.

This reorganisation of Germany can be achieved only if the deleterious selfish doctrines of democracy are first swept out with "an iron broom." (p.120) All the public licentiousness and vulgarity masquerading as "freedom" must be eradicated with "a strong-fisted

---

1903.

68 Since the nation is already determined by its racial and linguistic constitution, the reader may not confuse the reference to the multiplicity of the organic state with the multi-culturalism of a modern democratic one.

69 Now most fully typified by the herd-mentality of the Americans, who quickly reduce every aspect of society into its dullest, lowest common denominator.

70 cf. Chamberlain's elaboration of this theme in 'Deutsche Freiheit' in *Kriegsaufsätze*, München, F. Bruckmann, 1914, 'Deutscher Friede' in *Neue Kriegsaufsätze*, München: F. Bruckmann, 1915, and *Demokratie und Freiheit*, München: F. Bruckmann, 1917.

German revolt against the rule of the common people."[71] Not rights but moral duties are to be cultivated in the new German state since morality and wisdom elevate both the individual and the state. The duties of the people henceforth must include political service, whereby advisory committees on any particular social question are constituted of citizens who are enrolled on a rotating basis according to their expertise and given the opportunity to deliberate on political matters in conjunction with the administrative departments of the government. This system will preempt the undue power of professional parliamentary politicians who, as in the case of England, rule as a ministerial oligarchy and have little understanding of or sympathy with the welfare of the nation as a whole. In this reorganization of the state according to a more natural scheme of things, Chamberlain shows himself once again a disciple of Herder, who had also wished the dissolution of the state as an administrative "machine" of government and the substitution in its stead of an "organic" ordering of society. Active political participation based on talent and learning was ensured in Herder's system through the ad hoc institutions which would replace parliamentary processes.[72] In Chamberlain's project, the political service that an educated person renders should even become a condition of the suffrage, for one who has not proved himself capable of politics cannot influence its course. All the decisions of the advisory committees will, besides, be conducted not in the vulgar publicity encouraged by democracy, but to the express exclusion of the public. Only this will ensure that the wisest decisions will be taken and implemented without unnecessary external interferences and delays. In fact, Chamberlain points out that the conditions for a "self-administration" already exist in Germany since the administrative bodies are genuinely public ones and considerations of party politics do not hinder the establishment of efficient and appropriate laws.

Furthermore, the truly enlightened ideal of a human state built on Kantian inner freedom, or self-discipline, is already present in the

---

71 In his essay "Deutschland als führender Weltstaat", *Kriegsaufsätze* (München: F. Bruckmann, 1914), Chamberlain describes the people as the "unconscious root, supplying the nutriment, the reserve of the forces - As soon as the people are brought to silence, their voice is most distinctly heard - A monarch may be represented, a class, a profession - a people cannot be represented. The people are nature - This pretended representation of the people does nothing but destroy the real vigor of the people and cause a chaos - It stultifies by its debate and nullifies all great plans by its disputes" (tr. C.H. Clarke, in H.S. Chamberlain, *Ravings of a Renegade*, London; Jarrold and Sons, 1915, p.99 f).

72 Herder, *Werke*, ed. B. Suphan, XVII, p.127; cf. P.M. Barnard, *op.cit.,* p.86.

excellent organisation of the German army, in which every soldier, high and low, is united to his fellow through the obligation until death to the same national goal. In fact, the state will benefit greatly from emulating the example of the army since in it is represented the ideal of a society "in which everyone has his definite, regulated duties - not to chat about and assess things and overthrow majority decisions, but to settle according to instruction, and, if supreme efficiency has been practically confirmed, to perfect with insight" (p.129). Only in such a state, and not - as is commonly believed - in a democracy, will the truly philosophical ideals of freedom, equality, and fraternity be finally and fully realized.

IV: The legacy of Chamberlain:
The Neoconservatism and Prussianism of Spengler,
Moeller van den Bruck, Jung and Rosenberg

The immediate popularity of Chamberlain's *Political Ideals* has already been pointed to.[73] The significance of the work, however, is fully understood only when we see its continuance in the work of the neoconservatives, Oswald Spengler (1880-1936), Moeller van den Bruck (1876-1925), and Edgar Julius Jung (1894-1934),[74] and also - to a certain extent - in the political concepts of the Nazi ideologue, Alfred Rosenberg (1893-1946). That the neoconservatives were distinct from the National Socialists who followed them is evident from the fact that the former were primarily elitist thinkers whereas the latter were mostly a mass movement, as indicated by their designation as the 'Deutsche Arbeiter Partei', and one based predominantly on 'völkisch', or racialist, ideology. As Moeller van den

---

73 See above p.13.

74 Spengler, Moeller van den Bruck, and Jung are classified by Armin Mohler *(Die konservative Revolution in Deutschland, 1918-1932: Ein Handbuch,* 2nd. ed., Darmstadt: Wissenschaftliche Buchgesellschaft, 1972) as "young conservatives", and by Kurt Sontheimer *(Antidemokratisches Denken in der Weimarer Republik: Die politischen Ideen des deutschen Nationalismus zwischen 1918 und 1933,* München, 1964) as "revolutionary conservatives", so as to distinguish them from the National Socialists (see also K. von Klemperer, Germany's *New Conservatism: Its history and dilemma in the twentieth century,* Princeton: Princeton Univ. Press, 1957, and H. Gerstenberger, *Der revolutionäre Konservatismus,* Berlin: Ducker & Humblot, 1969).

Bruck himself made it clear, "The intellectual assumptions of the German revolution [i.e. the neoconservative revolution of the Weimar Republic] were formed outside National Socialism."[75] Similarly M.R. Gerstenhauer, a 'völkisch' writer of the thirties, declares that "We old 'völkisch' thinkers ... did not need to learn something in this field from new great men like Moeller van den Bruck or even Oswald Spengler, who were really not 'völkisch' at all." [76] The neoconservative movement, which was centered round the Deutsche Studentenschaft, the Deutscher Schutzbund and the Juniklub, in fact offered the most enlightened political program that Germany could have benefited from after the first Great War and the disastrous Weimar Republic. Although the members of this movement were numerous,[77] the thinkers discussed in this chapter are arguably the more representative and the most significant of them all.

Oswald Spengler's political views are best seen in his essay *Preussentum und Sozialismus* (1919), which was a sketch of the main themes of the second part of his two-volume *magnum opus, Der Untergang des Abendlandes* (1918 and 1922). Spengler's *Preussentum und Sozialismus* is in fact a repetition of Chamberlain's political ideals, which are now seen to be fully Prussian notions of the role of the state. The burden of Spengler's argument in this essay is the difference between the so-called Marxist socialism which is based on alien, English and Jewish, understandings of society and the genuine socialism of the Prussian state. In positing a radical distinction between the English sensibility and the German, Spengler was in fact following Chamberlain's lead.[78] The socialism of the English is demonstrated to be a Viking-like individualism which has encouraged the colonial rapacity of the British Empire and the mercantile ruthlessness of its leaders. The Norman conquest of England had put an end to the Anglo-Saxon way of life and introduced the 'piracy principle' whereby "the barons exploited the land apportioned to them,

piracy principle

---

75 Moeller van den Bruck, *Deutsche Rundschau,* June 1932, p.158.

76 M.R. Gerstenhauer, *Der völkische Gedanke in Vergangenheit und Zukunft,* Leipzig, 1933, p.63.

77 For more information on the neoconservative movement, see Armin Mohler, *op.cit.,* Kurt Sontheimer, *op.cit.,* K. von Klemperer, *op.cit.,* and H. Gerstenberger, *op.cit.*

78 In the *Kriegsaufsätze* (1914), for example, Chamberlain had discussed these differences in his essays, 'England' and 'Deutschland'.

and were in turn exploited by the duke."[79] The modern English and American trade companies are enchained to the same motives of profiteering:

> Their aim is not to work steadily to raise the entire nation's standard of living, it is rather to produce private fortunes by the use of private capital, to overcome private competition, and to exploit the public through the use of advertising, price wars, control of the ratio of supply and demand.[80]

The French democratic notions, on the other hand, are ruled by an anarchic love of pleasure since what every individual in the French state wants is "an equality of pleasure, equal opportunity for life as a pensioner." The Marxist doctrine, being a product of the Jewish mind, which is characterized by 'resentment', is based on an envy of those who have wealth and privileges without work, and so it advocates revolt against those who possess these advantages. It is thus essentially a negative variant of the English ethos. It is not surprising, therefore, that the worker in the Marxist doctrine is encouraged to amass his own profits through private business, so that, as Spengler puts it, "Marxism is," indeed, "the capitalism of the working class." The Marxist system is indeed the "final chapter of a philosophy with roots in the English Revolution, whose biblical moods have remained dominant in English thought."[81] The Marxian solution to boundless private property was only a negative one: "expropriation of the expropriators, robbery of the robbers."[82] On the other hand, Prussian socialism is

---

79 *Preussentum und Sozialismus,* in 0. Spengler, *Selected Essays* tr. D. 0. White, Chicago: H. Regnery Co., 1987, p. 82.

80 *op.cit.*, p.63.

81 *op.cit.,* p.97. What Spengler does not explicitly observe here is that the biblical mode of thought which directed Puritan capitalistic industry is in fact a basically Jewish voluntaristic one deriving from the conception of the universe as created by a Pantokrator who rules the creation with his Will as a personal Lord (See E. Zilsel, "The genesis of the concept of physical law". *Philosophical Review,* 51 (1942), 247ff, for a discussion of the Jewish origins of this concept, as well as Max Weber, *The Protestant ethic and the spirit of capitalism,* tr. T. Parsons, London: George Allen and Unwin, 1930).

82 *ibid.*

not concerned with nominal property, but rather with
techniques of administration ... The Old Prussian
method was to legislate the formal structure of the total
productive potential while guarding carefully the right
to property and inheritance, and to allow so much
freedom to personal talent, energy, initiative, and
intellect as one might allow a skilled chess player who
had mastered all the rules of the game. This is largely
how it was done with the old cartels and syndicates, and
there is no reason why it could not be systematically
extended to work habits, work evaluation, profit
distribution, and the internal relationship between
planners and executive personnel. Socialization means
the slow, decades-long transformation of the worker
into an economic civil-servant, of the employer into a
responsible administrative official with extensive
powers of authority, and of property into a kind of old-
style hereditary fief to which a certain number of rights
and privileges are attached.[83]

We have here a clarification of the political administrative method
outlined by Chamberlain in his *Politische Ideale.*
    The significance of the notion of the state is completely
ignored by Marx in his focus on 'society'. On the other hand, the
Prussian form of socialism is based entirely on the notion of the
primacy of the state, which is indeed the ideal of the Teutonic knight,
diametrically opposed to the roving plunder of the Viking:

The Teutonic knights that settled and colonized the
eastern borderlands of Germany in the Middle Ages had
a genuine feeling for the authority of the state in
economic matters, and later Prussians have inherited
that feeling. The individual is informed of his economic
obligations by Destiny, by God, by the state, or by his
own talent ... Rights and privileges of producing and
consuming goods are equally distributed. The aim is not
ever greater wealth of the individual or for every
individual, but rather the flourishing of the totality.[84]

---

83 *op.cit.,* p.ll9f.
84 *op cit.,* p.62.

While the English society is devoted to 'success' and wealth, the
Prussian is devoted to work for a common national goal:

> The Prussian style of living... has produced a profound
> rank-consciousness, a feeling of unity based on an ethos
> of work, not of leisure. It unites the members of each
> professional group - military, civil service, and labor -
> by infusing them with a pride of vocation, and dedicates
> them to activity that benefits all others, the totality, the
> state.[85]

The individual subsumed in the totality is however marked most
strikingly by "that glorious inner freedom, the *libertas oboedientiae*
which has always distinguished the best exemplars of Prussian
breeding."[86]

The administrative ideal that Spengler proposes for the
Prussian state is indeed very much like Chamberlain's:

> Let us envision a unified nation in which every one is
> assigned his place according to his socialistic rank, his
> talent for voluntary self-discipline based on inner
> conviction, his organizational abilities, his work poten-
> tial, consciousness, and energy, his intelligent
> willingness to serve the common cause. Let us plan for
> general work conscription, resulting in occupational
> guilds that will administrate and at the same time be
> guided by an administrative council, and not by a
> parliament.[87]

Parliamentarism is not only inappropriate in a monarchical state such
as the Prussian, but it is a tired and outmoded system which has lost
the glory lent it by the 'gentlemen' and aristocrats who once ruled
British and German politics. Now,

> the institutions, the sense of tact and cautious observance
> of the amenities, are dying out with the old-style people
> of good breeding ... The relationship between party
> leaders and party, between party and masses, will be

---

85 *op.cit.*, p.46.
86 *op.cit.*, p.40.
87 *op.cit.*, p.88.

tougher, more transparent, and more brazen. That is the
beginning of Caesarism.[88]

Selfish individuals employ democratic forms of parliamentarism to
make the "state" an executive organ of their own business interests,
"i.e. by paying for election campaigns and newspapers and thus
controlling the opinion of voters and readers."[89] Thus, democracy, in
general, is an unholy alliance of urban masses, cosmopolitan
intellectuals, and finance capitalists. The masses themselves are
manipulated by the latter two elements through their specific agencies,
the press and the parties.[90] The intelligentsia represent "abstract
intelligence," not spiritual enlightenment, while the finance capitalists
are supported by mobile fortunes distinct from the landed property of
the true nobility.

   In fact, the League of Nations itself is an instrument of big
business, and is "in reality a system of provinces and protectorates
whose populations are being exploited by a business oligarchy with
the aid of bribed parliaments and purchased laws."[91] As for the so-
called 'internationalism' of the modern Marxism, this is immediately
recognized as a sham when one notes the diversity of races and of
their responses to political movements. In fact, according to Spengler,
the true 'International' is "only possible as the victory of the idea of a
single race over all the others, and not as the mixture of all separate
opinions into one colorless mass."[92]

   The significance of Spengler's critique of English and Marxist
ethics cannot be exaggerated, for it serves as a reminder of the
importance of distinguishing between the English piracy principle and
the German state idea as well as between the false "socialism" of
Marx and the genuine one of the Prussian. The real meaning of
socialism, according to Spengler, is

> that life is dominated not by a contrast of rich and poor
> but by rank as determined by achievement and ability.
> That is *our* kind of freedom: freedom from the economic

---

88 *op.cit.*, p.89.
89 *op.cit.*, p.118.
90 See *The Decline of the West*, II, p.444; *Prussianism*, Ch. III.
91 *op.cit.*, p.118.
92 *op.cit.*, 111.

capriciousness of the individual.[93]

Ultimately, this is the same ideal that Chamberlain too had sought to convey to his German readers, and so we see that the ideas of Chamberlain were in fact consolidated in the writings of Spengler in the period between the two Great Wars. That Spengler was ostracized by the Nazis for his "pessimistic" outlook on history and for his criticisms of the Nazi dictatorship[94] is only ironical, since his spiritual kin, Chamberlain, was at the same time acknowledged as a "prophet" of the Nazi movement. Both Spengler and Chamberlain believed in the Prussian ideal of rule, not by popular parliamentary methods, but by an elite who would, like the military officer or bureaucrat, be characterized by devotion to duty and to the common good.

*

In the writings of Arthur Moeller van den Bruck (1876-1925) the Prussian ideal is crystallized as 'national' socialism, a concept which represents the pristine form of the Nazi movement. Moeller van den Bruck himself did not participate in a major way in the Nazi movement, even though the latter adopted the appellation of Moeller's political project, as well as the title of his book, *Das dritte Reich* (1923), for Moeller died by his own hand during a nervous breakdown in 1925. And, unlike the Nazi system, Moeller's was not predominantly racialistic. Moeller's vision of a Prussianized Germany conserving the living spirit of its national traditions through a strongly disciplined system of politics which involves the entire nation in its development at the same time as it champions the principle of a strong leadership and a hierarchical organization of the state is indeed very close to Chamberlain's ideals of politics.

Conservatism, as Moeller conceived it, is a pure form of socialism as well as of democracy since it involves the participation of the entire national community in the government. But popular representation will not be literal, as in a parliamentary democracy, but a system "based on the estates which shall assure us security and permanence." [95] Monarchy is the true basis of politics since it

---

93 *op.cit.*, p.130.

94 In his essay, *Years of Decision* (1933).

95 *Das dritte Reich*, 'Liberal', (tr. E.O. Lorimer, *Germany's Third Empire*, London: George Allen and Unwin, 1934, p.130).

represents "the power of a leader as example."[96] However, the old
monarchies, like that of Wilhelm II, who contributed to the ruin of
Germany through his association with the liberals, have become
dissipated and must be replaced by a more vigorous monarchy which
will "devote all their powers of decision, of will and of ambition to
securing the future of the nation."[97] A monarchy "must be fought for"
and the new monarch need not - as the 'reactionaries' maintain -
necessarily be a traditional aristocrat so long as he is a true leader of
the people and not a weak constitutional puppet. Moeller's view of the
leader is virtually that of a dictator, since, as he points out, "human
welfare cannot safely be left to human caprice, but can only be
attained by compulsion and leadership and the direction of someone
designated to supreme control."[98]

The chief enemy of conservatism is liberalism, since it is the
detested legacy of the French Revolution, which Chamberlain had
already criticized as the prime defect of modern politics. In fact,
Moeller's depiction of the liberal is very similar to Chamberlain's:

> The liberal is a mediocre fellow. Freedom means for him
> simply scope for his own egotism, and this he secures by
> means of the political devices which he has elaborated
> for the purposes: parliamentarianism and so-called
> democracy. Liberalism is only self-interest protectively
> colored.[99]

The system of parliamentarism is not a part of the "natural organic
structure" of the people since it is not in constant touch with them and
is utterly unsuited to Germany, where "the parliamentary system has
no tradition." Unlike Chamberlain, Moeller is not entirely anti-
capitalistic in his conservatism, since he considers the true capitalist to
be a "creator of values," whereas the real enemy is the profiteer, or the
rentier, who is a mere parasite. The socialist - from his characteristic
economic view - has already identified this enemy as the liberal, for
he is "the exploiter of the masses." In the mind of the conservative,
too, the liberal is "mentally a freebooter, politically a rationalist and a
utilitarian who can sneak in disguise into any form of government, can
destroy religion and has even been able to destroy conservatism."[100]

96 *ibid.*, p.226.
97 *ibid.*, p.228f.
98 *ibid.*, p.222.
99 *ibid.*, p.110.
100 *ibid.*, p.239.

Economics, in Moeller's conservative view, should be planned on a corporative basis focussed on the "idea of organization by trade and profession" as put forward by the Freiherr vom Stein.[101]

Communism too is only liberalism turned radical and revolutionary. Opposed to the communistic seduction of the people into the fallacious doctrine of class-warfare, Moeller maintains, like Spengler,[102] that the true socialist is a nationalist, since he devotes his entire work to the spiritual development of the nation. The Marxist conception of history is indeed basically defective, since it ignores the all-important spiritual dimensions of man for a limited focus on the physical and economic circumstances of the people. In this it resembles psychoanalysis, "a natural product of materialist thought," since both take "more pleasure in exploring man's shame than his glory."[103]

Moeller's view of historical development too is akin to Spengler's, but it significantly replaces the latter's pessimism with a more aggressive optimism. Unlike Spengler, Moeller does not consider history to be made up of predictable cycles of organic growth and decay of states but of spontaneous creative developments. And in Germany, this spontaneous force will manifest itself in military efforts to gain more land for its great population. Indeed, the bitter experience of the Great War made expansionism one of the major points of Moeller's political philosophy, for he considered the Germans, as a vigorous "young people," to be in natural need of the land towards the East.

*

Another significant thinker of the group of "young conservatives" that were associated with the 'Herrenklub' (the successor of the 'Juniklub' initiated by Moeller van den Bruck)[104] was

---

101 *ibid.*, p.74.

102 It may be noted, however, that, whereas Spengler favored August Bebel, the founder of the Social Democratic Party, as the true Prussian socialist, Moeller considered the genuine German socialism to be that of J.K. Rodbertus, the proponent of 'scientific socialism', and Wilhelm Weitling.

103 *ibid.*, p.55.

104 Oswald Spengler was also a member of the Munich branch of the Herrenklub in the 1920's (see his letter of July 7, 1925, to Werner von Alvensleben, *Briefe,* p.396).

Edgar Julius Jung (1894-1934), whose enormous work, *Die Herrschaft der Minderwertigen* (1929) is a detailed project of a new German aristocracy which would revive the socio-political ethos of the Middle Ages to combat the ills of the weak, liberal Weimar republic that was forced on Germany after the first Great War. Like Chamberlain, Jung begins with the negative ideal of individualism which characterizes the French Revolutionary liberal ethic and then goes on to portray the truly German, organic, form of the state. Jung decried the democratic notion of equality as "that political plague of the West,"[105] for it forms not a real community (Gemeinschaft) but only an artificial society (Gesellschaft),[106] for the former is always based on a hierarchical ranking of its members. In a democracy, the common man, characterized by resentment of all forms of superiority, perpetuates the rule of mediocrity. By granting equal rights to all and sundry, democracy will lead to a chaos of mutually opposed individuals, that is, to total anarchy. Self-interest takes the form of material interests, and economic values predominate to the extent that "financial pirates" manipulate the entire institution of democracy through political parties.

The functional differentiation of the members of a society which is a consequence of the natural inequality of men makes hard labor inevitable for the vast majority of the people since this is a psychological fact of life:

> According to a well-known law of economics even the most amazing inventions do not reduce the amount of toil and drudgery; at each ascending level, human demands increase. With each succeeding step, the external picture becomes more splendid, but the internal expenditure of toil, misery, and effort on the part of the great mass of men for their indispensable daily bread remains the same.[107]

---

105 The 'West' was the customary form of reference to the Revolutionary politics emanating from France.

106 These terms are borrowed from Ferdinand Tönnies' *Gemeinschaft und Gesellschaft*, Leipzig, 1887.

107 *Die Herrschaft der Minderwertigen*, Berlin: Verlag Deutsch Rundschau, 1930, p.436.

This fact (also emphasized by Treitschke) [108] is, however, made tolerable by the sense of commitment that each member of the society may have to his own work. Thus, even the political leaders of the corporative bodies will perform their offices without remuneration, unlike professional politicians. And if landed property is considered an appropriate qualification for a leader, it is only because "The independence of the rich man may even divert his concern for his person to a concern for the whole."[109] The economic institutions of an aristocratic state are best constituted corporatively, as they were in the Middle Ages.

The inequality of individuals also betokens, on a larger political scale, the inequality of nations. Spiritually, Germany is superior to all others and should conduct the spiritual revival of Europe. In this Jung is similar to Chamberlain, who insisted that it was the duty of Germany to ennoble the world.[110] Jung does not stress race as a factor of national development as much as the 'völkisch' thinkers of the National Socialist movement since eugenics seemed to him a materialization of racialism, which should be based on spiritual qualities and not on blood. It is the duty of the nation to preserve the best type of races, even if mixed, and to deter the worst. It is on this spiritual basis, and not on that of purity, that Jung distinguishes the Jews as a deleterious race devoted to individualism and its social variants, liberalism and artificial 'collectivism':

> It is true that the Jews are individualistic and therefore the people born to collectivism. They have little understanding of the Faustian battle for inner freedom... The notion of immortality, one of the demands of practical reason in Kant, is among the Jews transferred from the metaphysical realm to the this-worldly.[111]

---

108 See above p. 23f.

109 ibid., p.171f.

110 See, for example, 'Kaiser Wilhelm II' in Deutsches Wesen, München: P. Bruckmann, 1915, pp.23-33. It may be mentioned here, that, although Jung is in agreement with the medieval, Prussian, forms of statecraft, he, like Constantin Frantz before him, considers the Prussian hegemony since the time of Bismarck as a hindrance to the realization of a 'grossdeutsche' nation. For it makes of the German Reich a mere 'kleindeutscher "Staat"'. Like Frantz, too, Jung considers federalism to be the best form of national constitution.

111 Jung, op.cit., p.122.

Jung considered the liberal notion of 'freedom' as mere individualism typified by self-will, and the very opposite of true freedom, which is indeed "the creative power towards the divine life" arising from a consciousness of the unity of all the individual parts in an organic social and political whole.

In an organic state, unlike in a liberal one, even democracy will manifest itself as an aristocracy, and not as a confusion of conflicting political parties. The system of elections in a democracy which is instituted to periodically demonstrate the confidence of the people in the government is in fact a betrayal of the lack of confidence of the led in their leaders. The mechanical way to democracy, that is, through vote-majorities, leads to anarchy, whereas an organic state will represent its democratic ethos through a "faith in a social-ethical minority standing far above, which embodies in itself the highest spiritual-intellectual form of the state."[112] The organic state, thus, will be governed as an aristocracy, that is, as a "Herrschaft der Besten." Like Lagarde, Jung regarded the existing aristocracy of Germany to be unsuited to the tasks demanded by the new Reich and suggested that they should be replaced by a new aristocracy similar to the enduring British ruling class. While the true leader will generally be characterized by his birth, education, and inherited property,[113] the surest criterion of the ruling class is its commitment to society as a whole and to the duty of governing it.

The new Reich will, as a whole, be ruled as a well-disciplined army. The people have only one right - "to be ruled well"[114] and must look to the leader for direction, since he alone "determines the actions of the led as well as his own actions." However, the administration of the state will at all levels be characterized by a certain degree of autonomy, exactly as in Chamberlain's ideal state. Also, in spite of the almost unlimited power granted to the aristocracy by Jung, the latter will be an open one insofar as qualified men from the public will also be allowed to join it once they have demonstrated excellence in social and economic activity, though those who are merely adept at party politics will be excluded. The aristocracy of the new Reich will therefore be the truest form of democracy since it will not be based on the foolish weight of numbers but on the expression of the true will of the people, that is, of that social will directed towards the common, rather than the individual, good.

It is not surprising that Jung was opposed to Hitler's national

---

112 *Ibid.*, p.332.
113 *Ibid.*, p.328.
114 *Ibid.*, p.344.

socialist movement since it too was, according to him, only a nationalist form of liberalism which relied on mass appeal,[115] and, as Jung declared, "A new culture never begins with the unleashing of mass instincts, but only with their suppression."[116] Although Jung admitted that the Hitlerian movement served a limited purpose in destroying the alien political form of the Weimar republic, he was ultimately forced to consider Hitler's methods as unsuited to creating the new nobility of the organic state that he himself envisaged. His consequent criticism of the Hitler regime cost him his life in the 'Röhm purge' of June 1934. It is indeed unfortunate that the aristocratic anti-democratic ideas of Jung were thwarted so early, for they represented the best path that German conservatism might have followed after the debacle of the Weimar republic.

*

The influence of Chamberlain on Alfred Rosenberg (1893-1946), the chief Nazi ideologue, too, is a significant one, for Rosenberg himself admitted that his reading of the *Grundlagen* at the age of nineteen in Riga had a profound impact on his mind and inspired him to continue the crusade begun by Chamberlain for the German cause.[117] Though Rosenberg followed in Chamberlain's path, it cannot be said that the Nazi regime as a whole succeeded in realizing the political aims outlined in the *Politische Ideale*.[118] Rosenberg declares in his book on Chamberlain, *Houston Stewart Chamberlain als Verkünder und Begründer einer deutschen Zukunft,* that the economist Gottfried Feder had specifically incorporated Chamberlain's notion of directing economics from above - through nationalization of financial institutions, the regulation of credit, and the use of profits to reduce taxation and fund social reforms - into the Nazi party program of

---

115 See 'Bericht aus dem Deutschen Reiche', *Schweizer Monatshefte,* X (April 1930), p.39.

116 "Bericht aus dem Deutschen Reiche", *Schweizer Monatshefte,* X (Oct. 1930), p.323.

117 See G. Field, *op.cit.,* p.232.

118 This is not surprising since Rosenberg's political views themselves were often at variance with the ideas of Hitler, though Rosenberg, as an official of the Nazi party, was forced to follow the policies of the latter (see R. Cecil, *The Myth of the Master-Race: Alfred Rosenberg and Nazi Ideology,* London: B.T. Batsford Ltd, 1972).

January 1920.[119] But in general, the political ideals of Rosenberg, and Hitler, are characterized more exclusively by the primacy of race and racial honor as the foundation of the new state than those of Chamberlain were. For example, Rosenberg transforms the ideal of freedom so important in Kant, Fichte, and Chamberlain, into a race-bound ideal:

> A genuine organic freedom is possible only within such a [racial] 'type'. Freedom of the soul, like freedom of personality, is always form. Form is always plastically limited. This limitation is racially conditioned. This race is however the external form of a certain soul.[120]

This emphasis on the blood and the soil leads Rosenberg to denounce what he describes as the Jewish urbanistic commercialism of the present day, and to call for a return to the original, agrarian ethos of the German people. However, Rosenberg does follow generally in the tradition of Chamberlain and Spengler in considering the mission of the Nazis to be that of modern day "Prussians":

> The National Socialists are the Prussians of the 20th century. For, after the Thirty Years' War, Brandenburg[121] rescued the substance of the Germans from honorless princes and conveyed it through Frederick the Great into our times. Our desire is not to force German forms and German thought on other peoples, but we want to remind ourselves of ourselves and guard our culture for ourselves.[122]

In "Der deutsche Ordenstaat," Rosenberg returns to the social system of Teutonic medievalism to descry the first characteristic formation of the German state:

---

119 A. Rosenberg, *Houston Stewart Chamberlain als Verkünder und Begründer einer deutschen Zukunft,* München, 1927, p.54.

120 A. Rosenberg, *Der Mythus des zwanzigsten Jahrhunderts,* München: Hoheneichen Verlag, 1939, Bk.III, Ch.3, p.529.

121 The March of Brandenburg, the original Brandenburg-Prussian potentate.

122 "Deutsche Wiedergeburt", in *Blut und Ehre: Ein Kampf für deutsche Wiedergeburt,* München, Zentralverlag der N.S.D.A.P., 1934, p.263 (my translation).

> Not an impersonal official hierarchy, nor a Caesar who
> felt himself to be a god, hovering at an unapproachable
> distance, realized itself as the state conception of the
> German man, but the personal relationship between
> liege-lord and vassal became the most important
> element of the life-form ... Wherever this relationship
> was alive, wherever a relationship of a personal oath
> and duty existed, there was Germany strong, where
> however abstract theories began to rule there was
> Germany inwardly worn down.[123]

The same close association and devotion that prevailed between the
medieval duke and his subjects is to characterize the relationship
between the Führer of the modern nationalist movement and the
people. Neither a monarchy nor a republic, the new state will be a
"state of the German Order":[124]

> The National Socialist movement [has] resolved ... to
> select and join together, from the total of 70 millions, a
> core of men which have the special delegated task of
> state leadership, whose members grow into the notion of
> an organic politics from youth onwards, try themselves
> in the form of the political party, then strive together for
> that which is certainly not only possible to be realized on
> earth in every individual case but which must
> nevertheless remain the unshakable goal of the whole: to
> feel authority and proximity to the people as identical
> and to shape life and state accordingly.[125]

Although the centralization of power in the Führer and the medieval
form of the state make the new form of government virtually a
monarchy, it will be "a monarchy on republican foundations."[126] Like
Chamberlain, Rosenberg insists on service to the state as a
prerequisite for political participation, rather than the universal
suffrage of democratic parliamentarism without responsibility. Talent
rather than economic or social situation is to determine a person's

---

123 "Der deutsche Ordenstaat", in *Gestaltung der Idee,* München: Zentralverlag
der N.S.D.A.P., 1936, p.75 f.

124 The term is derived from the appellation of the medieval rule of the Prussian
Knights of the Teutonic Order.

125 *op.cit.,* p.79 f.

126 *op.cit.,* p.80.

contribution to the political career of the country. [127] The German "Order" would consist of men who had distinguished themselves by "achievements in the service of the nation," no matter in what field, and this Order would elect the leader of the nation, from its own ranks, for life. The parliament would be transformed into an advisory body to the government and would be made up of individuals elected, on the sole "principle of personality," by the leaders of corporative bodies such as the army, peasants' associations, businessmen, university professors, bureaucrats, and other liberal professions. The local chapters of the Order, such as the guilds, would also be able to nominate candidates to the parliament. This process would ensure the rise of "creative individuals" within the disciplined system organized by the Order and the leader of the nation.

The Nazi movement is thus seen by Rosenberg as a revival of the Prussian spirit which will finally ensure the continuance of the older, genuinely German, forms of government through the preservation of the soil and the blood of the people who constitute the state. However, as we know, the Third Reich was an abortive political project that was abruptly curtailed at the end of the second Great War. It is therefore useless to speculate what the planned German state may have been if Germany had won the war, and whether the Prussian ideal of Chamberlain and the revolutionary conservatives would have been given a chance of survival or not. Still, the significance of Chamberlain's criticisms of the shallow French Revolutionary ideals as well as of his focus on the German conception of freedom and the organic life of the nation remains as a powerful reminder of the extraordinary political potential that Germany possessed in the first half of this century.

---

127 Rosenberg, *Mythus*, Bk.III, Ch.3, p.546 f.

Houston Stewart Chamberlain

Political Ideals

Let the past be put behind us!
Goethe
[*Faust,* Part II, Act III, Scene 2]

Dedicated respectfully to a Prussian nobleman,
the inheritor of a historic name

I

In darkness presses the future forward;
The next future moment itself does
                                    not appear
To the open gaze of the sense,
                    of the understanding.
                                    (Goethe)[128]

    Politics observed from the standpoint of a narrower horizon is basically different from that politics which encompasses the wider horizon: for the former, the statesman, the general, diplomatic deception or the victorious war, is decisive, and assiduous boys and girls do well to imprint on their resistant mind lists of kings and popes with birth- and death-dates; in the latter, the statesman does not make politics; rather, politics makes itself, from itself, that is, without consciousness that it is politics, without battles and treaties and seals, without one's being able to put one's finger on the "who" and the "where" and the "when": "See, it was he there, and it happened there, and on that day was it accomplished." A thought of Kant's suffices to illuminate the relationship clearly: he differentiates between "man as nature" and "man as freedom": there we have the two horizons, and politicians as well as historians would do well to always differentiate between the two both in thought and in speech.

    Man "as nature" is man insofar as he belongs to an unlimited whole of nature; man "as freedom" is the same man considered as an

---

128 [*Die Natürliche Tochter,* Act V, Sc.7. Throughout this edition, my annotations, as distinct from Chamberlain's own, are given in box-brackets].

isolated personality; we all belong to both. Man "as nature" does not
know his own significance, he does not know either whence he comes
or whither he goes, he imagines that he deals consciously from his own
authority, and is in reality a servant of the necessity of nature imposed
on him as well as on millions of others; in this way he accomplishes
deeds in common with men whom he does not know, with past and
future generations, deeds, whose range the present is incapable of
measuring and which therefore remains to himself only darkly
half-conscious. It may be difficult to younger people to find themselves
in this context, for their age is that of self-mastery; older men know
from the experience of their own life how often they discovered only
after years which way they had been led unconsciously on. Man "as
freedom" is Aristotle's "Zoon politicon" familiar to all of us;[129] to him
belongs self-will, ambition, crime, pride, cunning, but especially the
incalculable suggestive power of the great personality; his works are
the conventions, the arrangement of treaties, the proclamation of laws,
the written state constitution, the declaration of war and the peace
congress, in short, all that makes up current politics and of which
history judges. Man "as nature" reaches deeper beyond and higher
above: he operates with necessity, like every natural power; what one
does not perform another performs, for the individual serves here, he
does not command; an Alexander and a Richelieu do not possess much
more of significance vis-à-vis this power than just any stone-cutter; it
sweeps everything before it, destroys or raises up; and only in its
operations does man manifest himself "as freedom." To it belongs - to
give only one example - the entire way of cultivating a country: what
should be raised and in what way attended to; here do states create the
possibility for growth in all fields, here are they fatally attacked until
they disappear; for example, if, in the course of the last forty years -
apart from the confusion of the senseless political bickerings - the
productivity of the German soil in relation to that of all other countries
had not powerfully risen, the German kingdom would not have been in
a position to nourish itself now during the world war by its own
products.[130]

   But this example occurs to me at this very moment; let us linger

---

129 [Political animal, Aristotle, *Politica*, 1253a7].
130 Cf. [Karl Theodor] Helfferich, *Deutschlands Volkswohlstand,* 5th edition, p.54,
and [Franz] Eulenberg, *Das Geld im Krieg,* p.50. Thus a hectare of corn in
Germany bears twice as much as in France, one and a half times as much as in
Austria, four times as much as in Russia.

here. We shall acquire breadth, depth and clarity.

The greatest revolution in the life of man on earth must doubtless have been produced by the introduction of corn cultivation. The idea of raising corn gives evidence thousand times more of genius, demands thousand times more inconceivable creativity of the imagination and conceals in itself thousand times more significance for the history of the human mind than any of the famed inventions and discoveries of our day. To be sure, neither child nor adult ever knows anything of it; we take corn, as we take the sun, for a natural given; and yet it is an invention of man, and indeed a "collective invention," doubtless developed by ingenious individuals, yet impossible without the wonderful presentient cooperation of the entire race, It is a work of man "as nature," and indeed a distinguished "political" work (in the wider sense of the word), for nothing has worked deeper and more transformingly on the conditions of life of peoples and nations. This idea must have been realised thousands of years before the oldest products of human culture preserved for us, and then continuously and steadfastly cultivated by thousands of generations following one another; for, no wildgrowing grass in the entire world bears this rich blessing of produce: rather, it must have been first cultivated; and the slow development to forms ever richer in produce, from the pile-dwellings and the earliest Egyptian evidence to the present, shows that that relative increase of produce, which we find there already, must have demanded thousands of years as well. How often may war, wandering, elemental catastrophes have destroyed the still tottering beginnings! But man "as nature" always began again from the beginning; the troublesome opportunistic politics of those early days - presumably even as complicated and wickedly arbitrary and diabolically self-seeking as that of yesterday and today - could slow down and stop its great cultural work temporarily, but it could not destroy the god-willed work indispensable for the existence of coming generations: the politics of the corn cultivators finally won the day and blessed all time down to our earnest present, with its pristinely reasonable bread-cards, in opposition to which the chronicle of kings and chancellors of that decisive past has thankfully been entangled in darkness and our tortured memory not burdened with further useless names and dates. Similarly does it transpire in the case of all that presents us nourishment and strength for labour. Anyone who takes up a few books on prehistory, such as Alphonse De Candolle's *Origine des plantes cultivées,*[131] Viktor Hehn's *Kulturpflanzen und Haustiere,*[132] Darwin's *Animals and Plants,* [133] Keller's *Ursprung unserer Haustiere*[134], Heinrich Schurtz's *Urgeschichte der Kultur*[135] will be surprised what a world of the unknown opens up before him. Cows which issue a thousand times more milk than their calves need, hens which lay eggs daily, pigs which, instead of remaining nimble and slim, build up their body with gross flesh and fat, horses destined to draw wagons and to bear burdens on their back - all of these are conquests which man "as nature" has wrung from his Mother and thanks to which the man of today as citizen of a state seeking on principle to preserve peace first became possible. We are wont to speak of cultural history in opposition to political history; however, if cultural history - as it happens in the case of Lamprecht[136] and his pupils - is included in political history, than we discover that here the more powerful creative form of politics is at work, the one which kneads and molds the other, destroys its hallowed traditions and forces new ways on it.

If one considers things on the basis of the really essential, then one discovers that thus almost everything that prepares the way for the life of life, that creates the conditions of our social existence and then transforms them again - basic perspectives, basic instincts, raw material, economic relations, art forms, thought orientations -stems from here. Thus, for example, has our modern technology and industry revolutionized, in the course of hundreds of years all of the life of the nations, placed them before entirely new political scientific tasks which not the narrower politics but the broader one of man "as nature" has created, so that our state authorities and politicians only lag and limp behind fully incapable - up to now - of seizing the leadership for themselves, since they are incapable of grasping the problem in its

---

131 [Alphonse de Candolle, *Origines des plantes cultivées,* Paris: F. Alcan, 1886].

132 [Viktor Heyn, *Kulturpflanzen und Haustiere,* Berlin: Gebrüder Borntraeger, 1874].

133 [Charles Darwin, *The variation of animals and plants under domestication,* London: J. Murray, 1868].

134 [Konrad Keller, *Die Stammesgeschichte unserer Haustiere,* Leipzig: B.G. Teubner, 1909].

135 [Heinrich Schurtz, *Urgeschichte der Kultur,* Leipzig: Bibliographisches Institut, 1900].

136 [Karl Gotthard Lamprecht (1856-1915), author of the multi-volume *Deutsche Geschichte,* Berlin: Weidmann, 1894-1909, and *Moderne Geschichtswissenschaft; fünf Vorträge,* Freiburg im Breslau: H. Heyfelder, 1905].

peculiarity. This rise of fully new conditions of life is not the work of this or that man; neither the Marburger Professor Papin, nor the Englishmen Watts and Stephenson, nor the Frenchmen Jacquard and Thimonnier, nor Gauss and Weber and Slaby and a thousand others are the original creators of them, since the inventions of these men would not generally have entered into the realm of possibility - without the clarion-call of great thinkers who since the 13th century, demanded a new kind of observation of nature - opposed to the ancient - without the awakening by the world voyagers of the 15th century, without the passion for pure mathematics which burst forth suddenly in the 16th century, without the series of physical theoreticians and experimenters in the 17th century and of chemical ones in the 18th century. None of these researchers and discovers were aware of the influence that they would exert through their works on the life and thought of men. Exactly as in the case of the world-revolutionizing idea of corn cultivation, do we stand here too before a total phenomenon, before a fully unconsciously manifested performance of man "as nature." If the poor individual man "as freedom" was also often enough scorned for the allegiance which he rendered to man "as nature," and tortured and murdered and driven to death by hunger - the total phenomenon of man "as nature" proceeded undistracted on its way, supported by no king, by no chancellor, by no parliament; and one day there appeared a new world which threw millions of men from the fresh air into the glow of the factory, made beggars of rich men, and millionaires of poor, which destroyed national values and called up others from the void into life, created new needs and with that new work, new intellectual stimulation, new benefits, but also new ambition and new envy and new misery, which brought in inroads compared to which those of Alexander seem insignificant, brought about the destruction of entire peoples and also made possible new wanderings of people across the oceans, overcame every distance and dispersed almost every trusted quiet proximity - which otherwise would have bound a man to other men from the cradle to the grave ...

Here too, once again, just one example, thrown in cursorily, and with the main aim of making the reader aware how great the power of ideas is in this man "as nature" who creates the foundations of all political life and, with that, its framework. It is entirely directive. If we may picture to ourselves at a very primitive stage the first planting of a wild-grown form of *Triticum*[137] for the purpose of obtaining wheat

---

137 [wheat].

seeds, this undertaking ushers in a completely incomprehensibly powerful idea, a true ideal, and one understands it if the ancient peoples held the plough to be a gift sent down from heaven by God! How should a man - instead of capturing fat spoils or ravaging roots and fruits - chance on the idea of cultivating tiny seeds - then incomparably tinier than today and in smaller numbers of scanty ears - while he gives himself the rash hope that in this way he would, in time, obtain abundant and safe food?[138] These men must have stood high above the practical men of their time; they must have been deeply religious enthusiastic natures with penetrating understanding and glowing ardor of faith. However, men like Roger Bacon and Descartes - to pick out only two names - who prepare the way for our new scientifically and technically transformed world, in that they destroy the classical viewpoint of an anthropocentric nature and show new ways, are related to these: It is ideas that lead them, ideals that command them, without their being able to predict that which will arise from them and which we only today gaze upon. Even if Descartes may, when we observe him in the perspective of the Church of his time, appear as a skeptic and opportunist, as the instrument of man "as nature," he belongs to the most pure idealists and fanatically faithful. This is not less valid however of Galilei and Kepler, of Gilbert and Boyle, of Stahl and Lavoisier. And if thousands and more had not worked together drawn by the same ideas, these more significant individuals would not have arrived at any transformation of civilisation with their accomplishments. Man "as freedom" may make do without ideals, to man "as nature" they are indispensable, they are the lodestars on his way into the unknown.

And let another thing be remarked further: the politics of man "as nature" does not merely build, it destroys what has been built and changes blooming lands into deserts. These things also do ideals effect. One sees what the Turkomans have made of the valleys of the Euphrates - the oldest and the richest corn land of the world! One looks at the bald mountains of Italy: upto the very top of the peaks, traces of earlier cultures show themselves; the Apennines must have offered to the gaze an extremely charming garden-grove; now the naked rock stares out, or it is covered by rocky soil on which only a few blades of

---

138 To avoid misunderstandings I observe here that it is known to me, namely from the work of Eduard Hahn, that the garden must have preceded the plough; however, the example does not lose its illuminating power through this. [See Eduard Hahn, *Von der Hacke zum Pflug,* Leipzig: Quelle und Meyer, 1914].

grass stand, scanty life-nourishment for lean young goats. Here social ideas, religious ideas, and the entire conception of the world cooperate: Italy, populated earlier by efficient tribes of north European parentage, has slowly become the booty of freed slaves from Asia and Africa, men without faith, without fidelity, without power. He whom a mountain trek leads from the canton of Bern to the canton of Wallis meets suddenly - without having noticed boundary-stones - well-kept ways on neck-breaking neglected paths, the most painstaking cleanliness of the remote cow-grazing Alps in begrimed dirt, health and good cheer in weak-minded and crippled people, beautiful racial culture in crass ignorance: the conception of the state is, on both sides of the watershed, exactly the same, it is a question of two branches of the same federation; the politics of man "as nature" is a different thing; and indeed it is not only different in race and religion, but different since it has been subjected in Wallis - although the dwellers originally and also now belong in part to the German language family - to Gallic influence, whereas the Protestant Berner, even as his Catholic neighbor of the original canton, upholds and preserves his German being.

Only now have we arrived where I wanted. For, on one side, we see that the ideals of man "as nature" are of incalculable and often fateful influence on the life of the state, on the other side arises the question in us why we should not have succeeded in perceiving these powers of man "as nature," these mighty, unconquerable powers, as scientifically clearly as we have learnt to perceive the other powers of nature - and even if it be only through symbolic attempts at approximation, with the result that we should have then succeeded, as in the latter case, in subduing and leading "nature" to a certain sense and measure, and in drawing it on in this way to accomplishments of which mankind - until now thrown here and there by weak-sighted transient interest-politics - neither knows nor divines the smallest detail? Thereby we would have then introduced a higher politics, indeed established a thoroughly new ideal of political efficiency. I believe that this new ideal is a pressing need, and even at the risk of being considered confused dreamers and even scorned, like the first corn cultivators, we should, without delay, try to seize it from the clouds of the future and lead it into the present.

We do not wish to be foolhardy, we do not wish indeed to imagine that railways, telegraph, air-ships, giant steamers, automobiles, aniline dyes, etc., etc., signify in and of themselves, in any sense of the word, a "progress" for mankind; increased means demand increased spiritual strength, otherwise man dwindles to a slave of his own machines:

> In the end, however, we depend
> On creatures that we made.[139]

In the villainous world of cunning, lies, cruelty, definite vulgarity and meanness, which shrinks from no crime, which became blatant as a concomitant of this war, even the blind man must learn to see whither the journey tends with all the praised achievements of the new age. "What help is it to a man if he gained the entire world and damaged his soul?"[140] Considered from the widest world-historical standpoint, I find a certain analogy between our present situation and that of that groping, seeking original ploughman. I say analogy, not similarity; for it is a precisely reversed situation: there the hard battle for bare existence enslaved the spirit, the soul lacked the instruments to be able to develop itself into a secure and blessed existence in peace; the man of today is threatened by the opposite danger: that, in comparison with the powerful, cosmically swollen instrumental apparatuses, the relatively much retarded spiritual powers break down. Man "as nature" is among us mighty in works: the new world, which bursts forth with uncanny haste from all sides, makes itself, we do not make it, man "as nature" does not make it; swept along unwillingly, we do not know if it happens through a heavenly whirlwind which will drag us atop mountain peaks or through a satanic whirlpool which will finally hurl us down into abysses. And I think that now a really scientific politics, a politics, that is, which has not limited itself to the opportunistic resolution of pressing current questions, but prudently examined and exactly comprehended what man "as nature" creates and what possibilities remain for the way ahead, could ascertain what must happen now, so that mankind may not dash against a sort of end-of-the-world collapse with a return to bestiality (as it has to all appearances), but that it may overcome this threatening mortal danger and grow towards a higher future in the honorable use of subjugated natural powers - to a slow but surely maturing and lasting spiritual benediction comparable to the harvest which the inventors of agriculture gifted for all time to our growing generation.

Now perhaps someone would interject here: "It is logically futile to want to transform the unconscious into consciousness; you have just shown us what an enormous power lies in the goal-unconscious effect of man "as nature," why should we content ourselves to leave mankind

---

139 [Goethe, *Faust,* II, Act 1, "Laboratorium"].
140 [Luke 9:25].

to obey the law of inner need in future in the hope that it, in spite of blind statecraft and of the fundamental unruliness of all the elements of the general commonality striving against the higher goal, will follow the right path with god-given power? Here rules the condition: "the honor is yours, but yours also is the labor." This method does not seem to me to be quite heroic; it does not stand on the heights of a "great age," of which we hear so much. Should the age thus be great, and we pathetic and sloppy and indolent and cowardly? And should something great finally emerge from this? No, that cannot be! There are decisive hours - as in the life of the individual, so also in the life of peoples - hours when it is a matter of willing. Such an hour has struck for Germany. Certainly the very first ploughmen were a sort of fools - so does the world call a man given to such an enthusiasm; as Paul has sharply expressed it, to the "natural man," generally, "that which comes from the spirit of God is a folly" (1 Cor., 2.14); and so, doubtless, to the "natural" or average man of that time, even the seeking for bread was a folly; for, the fact that man would become "man" only through his victory, that he did not consider, that he could not consider in his limited cleverness based on experience alone. Finally, however, the day dawned in which the wisdom and the blessing of this "folly" illuminated others too; and on this day must have arisen a long war; for now the equipoise between men tilted, indeed according to the politics that they followed: the hunters and robbers recognized the threat to their supremacy, the inventors of peace - for the cultivators are that - had to become soldiers, otherwise their work of peace would be destroyed with one blow. Each downfall into the basic conditions of life brings war with it. We see however exactly here the fundamental difference between war for plunder and war for justice and peace: two mutually alien political ideals maintain themselves here - as today, so then. However unconscious, in the case of such economic-political revolutionary movements, the fundamentals may remain in future, there comes, in the case of every world-historical event of this sort, a moment when, from the conflict of interests - and that means as soon as one learns to follow the concatenation far enough up to the conflict of interests - a life-and-death decision draws near; here then there is a command of duty to make one's deeds conscious to oneself: and to that is linked the notion that one should present one's ideals, one's ideas, and one's goals clearly before one's eyes as a confession, as thoughts, as a decision. Such a moment - so I think -is now here. And we are armed differently than men in earlier critical days ever were, for the purpose of obtaining a clear gaze and making decisions conscious of a goal.

It suffices however to present the context clearly, as I have tried now to do, so that one fact may immediately spring to the eyes: at the present moment, Germany alone among all the nations is capable of grasping this thought in a new orientation of human politics that follows a higher reason. Among other peoples, only some individuals would understand what we are talking about; to want to win the general public to it would be hopeless; the culture is lacking, the awareness is lacking, the will is lacking, even the advantages of the others stand in their way here, whereas, certain shortcomings of the Germans allow themselves to be turned into account. So, for example, is the complaint of "defective political foundation" often made against the German - and not unjustly; nevertheless, if a radical reaction occurs in the conception of what politics must be, if the German people create for themselves new ideals, not in dependence on ancient tradition and on foreign models, but rather from scientific sobriety and their own need, then will the German really manifest himself as the first politician of the world, since he will systematically embark upon, flexibly engage in, diligently operate and logically persevere. The present war has discovered an extremely deep opposition between the German conception of human value and, together with that, also of state value and the conception of this notion in most other countries of Europe, including the American variety. I take no account of the press and of professional politicians: these people fall involuntarily into exaggerations and propaganda; it is certain that even the morally serious, the sober, thoughtful citizens of the enemy states foster the conviction that they are fighting for civilisation and freedom against barbarism, thus also - as they often declare - for the redemption of a "better" Germany from the snares of a demonical bad Germany; of the sincerity of this conviction we have no right to doubt, and it helps little if we think to dispose of the matter with contempt alone. I believe, rather, that the new world, which man "as nature" has been erecting around us for some hundreds of years, has operated differently on Germans (discounting certain, for the most part foreign, parts) than on other peoples; thus there has been a conflict that increased in the last fifty years, on the one side manifestly, on the other side under the surface. The nations of the west and the south which the cultured classes of Russia follow have fallen increasingly into the region of influence of the ideas of the French Revolution which we may summarize in this manner: self-will of the individual, violence of those ruling, moral chaos - that they call "freedom" and "civilisation," and this ideal they feel is threatened by Germany. In the meantime, Germany (and what lies under German influence) has inwardly - in spite of millions of Socialistic voters, in spite of materialistic propaganda by professors, in spite of the conquest of the surface through Communistic mercantilism and frivolous corruption of morals - Germany has, I say, in the entirety of its productive and creative powers, as we become aware of it once again during the war, gone another way and has thereby ripened unconsciously to new political ideals whose essential monument will be that the scientific method from which the new environment of our world has arisen will be made serviceable through a spiritual mastery of the consolidation of the whole - therefore of the whole of the state - organized according to plan, so that each individual citizen may grow and thrive therein and, with him, the entire people. There the mechanizing of external life already encroached deeply into the inner life, through which, with certainty, either one or the other species of the pure military state has been introduced; here, however, the higher culture of the middle classes, but especially the inherited inner freedom which distinguishes the Germans, has counteracted that fateful influence. There, therefore, the orientation towards atomism and mechanism, here the orientation towards ordering and organism; there undisguised mammonism, here the primacy of work; there remorseless tyranny of the few under the appearance of a people's government, here among many cultivator-like energetic dreamers the conviction that, through the consolidation of long preserved forms, the state can be transformed from inside and, through wise restriction, real freedom be made possible for the first time; above all: there the ancient prejudice that mankind is the measure, here - newly taught - the attention to the voice of Nature in order to win a living kingdom of inexhaustible variety.

The further course of this essay should present the details of the basically different ideals over there and over here. At present I have to establish only in what sense we may say without exaggeration and without a trace of self-glorification: Germany is chosen. Germany is chosen to take over the leadership of itself and of the other nations in the world to salvation. Providence has prepared the destined people in the destined moment for the destined duty. The future of mankind depends on whether Germany is equal to this expectation - let us say calmly this destiny - or not. We do not stand here before the same problems as Bismarck; we can exercise and steel ourselves in his way, but we must stand on our own feet - that is what we have to learn above all from the mighty man; let us honour him in remembering his words: "It is in politics, if in any field, that faith manifestly moves mountains, that courage and victory are not in causal connection but identical." The entire old politics and diplomacy which is sacred to our court councillors and our privy councillors, our chancellors and ambassadors, the members of our State Parliament[141] and Imperial Parliament,[142] belongs as much to the ancestral lumber as astrology and alchemy: with one ounce of truth ninety nine ounces of nonsense, madness instead of knowledge, dogmas instead of observations, traditions instead of methodology, insane waste of time and power, in order to obtain with the most enormous expense the smallest result. There would have been no more youth in Germany if it had proceeded further in this manner! We must want the better, then will we win it too; if we do not want it, if we do not learn to want it, if our political life has fallen into senile paralysis, then will the worse, which increases, deluge us and carry us away into hell, where we belong. Only a clearly conscious conception of new political-social principles and decisive fearless following of these paths would ensure the final winning of the goal.

141 [Landtag].
142 [Reichstag].

II

Freedom is the hushed speech of secret conspirators,
The loud field-cry of the blatant revolutionary,
Indeed, the pass-word of despotism itself. (Goethe)[143]

The impotence of political systems and the - for better or for worse - indomitable might of political ideals: these two facts have proven to me in all historical studies and in all the observations during my own life as irrevocably certain. Napoleon, who held all triumphs in his hand, was vanquished since he had no ideals, only plans; armed with ideals he would have conquered the world; instead he had to succumb to the "ideologues" scorned by him.

For the most part, men inherit their political ideals and do well to hold on to them. If world-history has however brought forward great revolutions, if man stands in between two epochs, thus in a transition stage, as it is the case today where unrest has gripped all the peoples of the world and, even in the case of the cautious German, ferments everything and transforms itself with radical transformations which have assailed his fatherland, and thwart and attack the political efforts in such a way that nobody knows any more what he wants or what he should want, then enters the need for new, brightly burning, ideals in which a new age can recognize itself and according to which it can orientate itself. Now, precisely here most people stumble, since they do

---

143 [Goethe, *Noten und Abhandlungen* zu *besserem Verstandnis West-Ostlichen Divans,* Nachtrag I].

not know which step must be taken first that man may reach the daylight from the darkness. All seek for definite political plans - often very acutely thought out - but they remain finally in the old fixes or half-measures, even though they recognize their inadequacy since the planned innovations seem fantastic to them and thus frighten away the sober judicious person. This path is an abortive one; German ways have already for a long time made that clear; whoever takes it does not understand the strife between the self-will of the individual and the wisdom and power of Nature - even of moral-social Nature; once again, man "as freedom" wishes to dabble with bringing about man "as nature." At a turning point such as that of the present it is our first duty: to create free paths for the original power of Nature acting out of unconscious necessity. Now, this does not happen if we ask ourselves directly what we want; we must rather first of all be fully clear of what we do not want. Schiller says, "It is not therefore enough that something begin that was not yet; something must first stop that was." In the same sense and with special clarity, has Richard Wagner expressed himself, from whose social-political thoughts our leaders could learn much: "The individual cannot invent, but only get possession of the invention. We need only know what we do not want, then we may reach, out of involuntary natural necessity, quite certainly that which we want, which will become quite clear and conscious to us only then when we have reached it" *(Sketches, Thoughts, Fragments).*[144] The usual question, "What do you wish to establish then in the place of the rules of today?" is to be declined as premature; it seems very clever, but demonstrates in reality only a lack of sense; if our predecessors had all allowed themselves to be deterred by this objection, we would have possessed even today no bread, no vegetables, no dairy produce. Nature gives an answer only then when we have become fully clear about what we do not want.

Here, for my part, I answer with all certainty: what I do not want, what I definitely reject is the political ideal which rules the present world, namely the ideal of the French Revolution.

In the three words, "Liberté, Égalité, Fraternité" - freedom, equality, brotherhood - at first nothing dangerous seems to be present; who would not like to want the spread of such noble things? Nevertheless, they have - considered as a political ideal, brought forward as programmatic banners - sufficed to destroy a great nation

144 [See Richard Wagner, *Sketches and Fragments,* in *Prose Works,* tr. W.A. Ellis, London: Routledge and Kegan Paul, 1899, Vol. VIII, p.347f.].

down to the foundations of its political structure, so that nothing further remained from which a new conception of the state could arise and establish itself lastingly. Even today the kingdom created by the Franks is full of talent, not poor in energy and in inventive spirit; its courage still (even as I write these words) runs full-tilt heroically on the eastern frontier against the strong wall of the German will; yet, politically, it is destroyed forever, and only a repetition of a Frankish conquest could, if need be, wake it to new vital power; from it itself it cannot accomplish that, since all the best blood was sacrificed to its ideal, and since, besides, this destructive ideal has completely consumed the thought and feeling of the otherwise so clever Frenchmen - that which it calls, in one sorry word borrowed from American English, "la mentalité," as the worm [consumes] wood, so that no doctor can cure it and no engineer can restore it to its original condition. In the meantime these three words have operated farther from country to country: before our eyes, Italy is perishing, the other Mediterranean countries are threatened, England is already infected and rushes madly towards its political downfall; in Russia, the Revolution under the same field-cry is relentlessly at work and calls forth the counter-influence of Panslavism which threatens Teutonism as its only possible defence; most of the South American states live on the same principle in hardly uninterrupted anarchy, and whoever has eyes to see will not doubt that the United States and the English colonies will go sooner or later the same way.

This ideal "freedom, equality, brotherhood" - understood as it was understood of the French Revolution and as it has acquired a dogmatic currency in the heads of millions since then - is the broad gate, gleaming in a blinding fireworks of ten thousand phrases, the "Arc-de-Triomphe" through which mankind marches in the shortest way into chaos. And, indeed, for this reason that all the three parts of this ideal are lies, lies in the unlimited sense of the word, whereby I mean: opinions which directly contradict the truth of Nature. I do not deny that this attempt of man to want to go against eternal Nature, to say to her, "You want it so, I wish it otherwise," can temporarily charm one to astonishment; the one who defies power can be sure to win sympathy; however, if one goes to the bottom of the matter then one easily discovers Gallic insolence, nothing more; insolence born of shallow thought, united with aimless desire. The historical causes of the Revolution - the intolerability of the degenerate ruling class, the over-taxation of rural labour, the disarray of the finances, the corruption of the army - have little to say here: for, the real people - the suffering - did not invent this ideal; the people wanted bread, nothing more; hedge-lawyers and superficially learned men are the authors, and the bourgeoisie - supported by the lesser nobility bordering on the bourgeoisie - is, as generally, so also here, the bearer of the Revolution. This ideal did not spring from the soil, as a result of Nature operating with necessity; for, then, it would have possessed deep-reaching roots and would have revealed at every stage - even in the midst of the destructive process - creative power, whereas the definite sterility of this ideal has manifested itself every time and in every place in a frightful way.

First, all the three opinions are, as mentioned, lies against the truth of Nature. "Les hommes naissent et demeurent libres" - men are free from birth and remain free: that, however, is to scorn all reality. No animal on earth emerged into life so miserably needful of help as man: naked, weaponless, hairless, requiring devoted care for twenty years before he can think of standing on his own. Man is not born free, but born in definite dependence. As if that were not enough, man is, as a result of his weakness, his destitution, his poverty of instinct, an animal that is incapable of enduring in isolation; socialisation is a condition of his existence on earth; and socialisation means ever reciprocal duties and, therewith, limitation of the self-will of the individual; and since selfishness is an inborn instinct, the limitation appears mercilessly harsh in the simplest of the forms of state known to us. Neither prehistory nor history can report anything of a "free" man. On the contrary, freedom is a goal to be striven for, a final goal, which only a morally superior state can set for itself, and which can be imagined as reachable only analogously to Goethe's words, "externally limited, inwardly unlimited"; to ensure unlimited moral freedom for man would be the highest accomplishment of a strong, strictly articulated state; nowhere is true freedom ever more badly protected as in all of the democratic states. To make this conception, on the other hand, the political point of departure of a state - as the Revolution ideal wishes it - is a sheer nonsense, since it digs up the foundations of every state. Not greater in truth, but more striking to the eyes is the stupidity of the second opinion: "Tous les hommes sont égaux par la nature" - Nature sets all men equal. So it is not a question of equality before the law or equality in relation to responsibilities and duties, no: Nature has made all men equal to one another! That men are equal to one another in no respect, cela crève les yeux, as the Frenchman says, "it strikes the eyes." Neither with regard to height, nor to colour, nor to bodily strength, nor to facial features, nor to talent, nor to will power, nor to abundance of feeling is there equality between men, rather they differ from one another almost immeasurably. The teachers of the Revolution refer expressly to Jean Jacques Rousseau, though unjustly; for he too was a daring dreamer, it never occurred to him to maintain anything so nonsensical. The thesis of his famous *Discours sur l'origine de l'inégalité parmi les hommes* runs: indeed men are from birth equal, still do not, for that reason, pity man in a primitive condition, because there inequality cannot come into its own: "L'inégalité est à peine sensible dans l'état de nature et son influence y est presque nulle",[145] and now he shows that every socialisation of man - even the simplest family formation - and every development of his spiritual capacities, first of all every state formation, draws out ever more strongly the inborn inequality with inescapable necessity and lets it acquire significance; from which he infers that the naked savage, who possesses hardly the simplest rudiments of a language and recognizes neither the mother of his children nor his children "when he meets them in the wood," is the happiest man. If the representatives of the modern political ideal have the courage of consistency, then they must demand the dissolution of every state, every society, every culture; if they did that they could subscribe least of all to their ideal, and if they did not do it, however, then it would remain definite lies. Fraternity or - as Littré interprets the term - "the common love which unites all members of the human family,"[146] is already more inclined to corrupt sentimental souls. However, very unjustly; for, not love, but duty lies under the conception of the state. There can very well exist a state without love, namely without the communistic brotherhood, but no state can exist without the fulfilment of duty, subordination, obedience. Here also, again, as in the case of brotherhood and equality, it is a question of an ideal which shapes a goal worth striving for, not, however, of a possible fundamental political idea.

So much about the inner falsity of the three notions which reduce these ideals to a tricolour and which have driven so many millions of heads out of their political senses. But now there follows a second important consideration.

Freedom, equality, brotherhood have been meant by the champions of the Revolutionary ideal never affirmatively but, in reality, always and only negatively! Historically, indeed, they arise as

---

145 [See J.J. Rousseau, *Discours sur l'origine et les fondements de l'inégalité parmi les hommes* (1755), the conclusion of the first part].

146 [See Emile Littré, *Conservatisme, Révolution, et Positivisme,* Paris: Librairie philosophique de Ladrange, 1852, Part II, Ch.18: "Et quel progrès accompli de notre temps, et préparer une organisation d'abord europééne, et finalement universelle, dont les plus hardis penseurs dans le passé avaient pu à peine concevoir quelque ébauche!"].

negations, and their inventors immediately pass on to oppression, mass murder and civil war. Freedom, in the mouth of the Frenchman and of all taught by him, possesses generally no meaning that is conceivable positively; the notion changes into all colours; and since it is (as mentioned already) the essence of every state and since it constitutes the notion of a "state" to limit the self-will of the individual to the benefit of all, so an abrupt profession of "freedom" meant simply the announcement of anarchy: these people did not think so far, and those who parrot them today do not either, rather, the word freedom possesses for them the very simple and understandable meaning: I do not want to obey. Freedom means here the opposition to every politically ordering power and, in the wider sense, to everything which possesses significance and, in consequence of that, also worth and power. Similarly does it occur with the word "equality." The revolutionary leaders of yesterday and today did not think and do not think to destroy the state - their milch-cow - as Jean Jacques Rousseau, the dreamer, had wished; rather the field-cry "equality" also meant to them simply an easily understandable negation: I want to show no respect. A man may be ever so sacrificing, ever so distinguished, ever so heroic, his talent may radiate everything customary ever so brightly, he may save the fatherland in the hour of danger and in peace immortalise it through his works; I, just any fool and lazybones, I a coward, a base-minded egoist have decided to show him no recognition, no reverence, no gratitude. How precisely the true meaning of the word has been arrived at here the Revolution demonstrated when it dragged the most significant scholars and natural scientists of France and gave them to the guillotine: only in death are we all equal. And now "brotherhood," love! Everybody who knows the history of the French Revolution must laugh out loud at the thought that "love" should have been one of its protective goddesses. One whom the men who had seen and heard him could call no other wise than as the son of God has condensed the essence of genuine love in eternal words: "Love your enemies'" Love is giving, not taking. Quite differently is the "fraternité" of the old and new revolutionaries meant, namely in the sense of a negation: I love nobody who does not think exactly as I do.

Let us therefore translate the "holy original" of the arrogant fanfare, "freedom, equality, brotherhood" into our beloved, honest German, then it would sound as: "Do not obey, do not revere, do not love"; more powerfully put: "disobedience, irreverence, hate."

It is always worth the trouble to go to the bottom of things and not to rest until one beholds and looks through and has comprehended it completely clearly. Now we have no further need of any circumstantial arguments: if we know the ideal from which, in all states that are linked to the French Revolution, the fundamental principles have been derived, then we also know immediately which ways these states must necessarily wander: from the triple alliance of disobedience, irreverence, hate arises with necessity tyranny, mediocrity, heartlessness; whereby I mean: despotic government, oppression of the significant, deadening of the public body to iniquity and, generally, to injustice and suffering.

The French Revolution gave us precisely the proof of the rightness of our reckoning: the most immeasurable misuse of the despotic desire of ruling that history has ever seen. Yet, those who cannot be convinced may still complain that there it is a question of the inroads of the first moment, of the misuse of the Revolutionary ideal before the latter had time to work itself out. The consequence, however, has taught us better. One needs only to look at the present French government: under the device, "liberté, égalité, fraternité" the country is ruled by a clique of conscienceless professional politicians who - as the Frenchman and Republican Gustave Le Bon writes in the year 1913 - "by the word freedom understand the right to persecute their enemies as they will,"[147] who, if by chance a truly gifted and incorruptible politician appears, remove the inconvenient outsider simply through murder, and who are so entirely without any sympathy for the needy that France does not still possess the most decisive beginnings for an old-age and invalid pension and is, after Italy, that country of Europe in which the least is spent for the purposes of welfare. So also, however, is it in the other countries which have subscribed to this ideal. While there are still good dreamy Germans who enthuse about "English freedom," the English governmental principle in reality equals more and more a dictatorship. Already twenty years or more ago the clear-sighted Seeley called the English Prime Minister a "King" and indeed an "almost absolute";[148] to be sure, he can be overthrown by the Parliament; still, in the first place, the party discipline is draconically strict and the smallest majority suffices to subject the entire people to him; in the second place, however: if the majority changes, then another tyrant appears - nothing more; then can an end be made at any moment of every debate in Parliament through the so-called "guillotine paragraph" of the house rules,[149] and the Parliament becomes finally a mere coordinating device

---

147 [Gustave le Bon, *Aphorismes du temps présent*, Paris: E. Plammarion, 1913].
148 [John Robert Seeley (1834-95), author of *The Expansion of England*, 1883, *The growth of British policy* (1897), and *Introduction to political science* (1901)].
149 [In 'Deutsche Freiheit' *(Kriegsaufsätze,* München: F. Bruckmann, 1914),

- whose results are known beforehand; the upper house is now more a decorative ornament robbed of its political powers, and the King possesses no right of veto.[150] In the course of the 19th century - especially under the influence of the Jew Disraeli -England began to be increasingly unfaithful to its old political ideals which it had preserved from shipwreck for half a millennium, in spite of all the storms of time, and tended it to steady further development; since the accession to the throne of King Edward VII the ruling party opened its arms fully to the French Revolutionary ideals. As in all democratic states: men of outstanding significance find in English political life today no more room for activity, no recognition, no possibility of influence and withdraw themselves leaving their place to idle and - as the Marconi scandal has shown[151] - often already corrupt demagogues. The

Chamberlain refers to the 'guillotine' paragraph in the following manner: "The restriction of the freedom of speech, particularly by the introduction of the so-called "guillotine" which permits every debate to be broken off at a certain time and a vote to be taken at once, has transformed this pretended freest of all parliaments into a kind of machine, by means of which a small group of politicians rule and govern for seven years according to their own sweet will" (tr. C.H. Clarke, *The Ravings of a Renegade, being the War Essays of Houston Stewart Chamberlain*, London: Jarrold and Sons, 1915, p.51)].

150 I gladly take the opportunity to recommend warmly a short, quite excellent book which appeared recently: Professor Arnold Oskar Meyer's *Deutsche Freiheit und englischer Parlamentarismus* [München: F. Bruckmann, 1915]. The author shows that at all times Germany enjoyed more true freedom than England; in England freedom is apparent, in Germany real.

151 [The scandal involving a number of high ranking British politicians and the Marconi Wireless Telegraph Company. See the contemporary 'Report of the Select Committee of Inquiry', Part I, where it is declared that the allegations "ranged themselves under two main heads. It was stated or implied: *First,* that a member or members of the Government [i.e. the Attorney General, the Chancellor, and the Chief Ministerial Whip], acting in the interests of Marconi's Wireless Telegraph Company Limited — and in disregard of public interests, had exercised undue influence to procure for the Company a Government contract, or had, in some way, exercised improper or undue influence — in the course of the negotiations for such a contract; and *Secondly,* that a member or members of the Government, with a knowledge acquired in his or their official capacity of the nature of the negotiations and of the probability that an Agreement would be completed of great value to the [Marconi] Company, during the progress of the negotiations had purchased shares in that Company with a view to selling them at a profit on the announcement of a

enormous amounts of money which every election in England now costs show that the method of the United States has naturalised itself: of buying votes. And thereby one may not forget that England was the most "conservative" people holding fast most tenaciously to tradition; this still distant movement has therefore not penetrated the entire people; so the picture there is not yet so clear as in France and in Italy; yet, the downward rolling movement now proceeds so terribly rapidly that catastrophe already dawns visibly on the horizon.

I shall not say more on this; the fiasco of the Revolutionary ideal is too blatant; one needs only to open one's eyes and to look around one. Few, however, penetrate to the causes and obtain the understanding that political downfall is the inevitable consequence of false political ideals and, all over the world where these ideals find entry, it will necessarily occur all the time. The so-called "freedom" reduces men to atoms, "equality" makes them faceless counters, so that one values them now more according to the weight of their money purse, "brotherhood" quenches love and compassion. The Frenchman is not a "worse" man than the German, rather he possesses, apart from moderately good talent, excellent characteristics; not corruption and not impotence have caused the downfall of his state but, in the final analysis, the devotion to basically inverted political ideals which are opposed to all the healthy ideas of state in the minds of the citizens, Precisely in the time of the Revolution have the otherwise sober and cautious French people brought forth enthusiasts, fanatics, idealists, people who believed in all seriousness that they would reform the world and make men happy. However, ideas work with natural necessity and with elemental power as soon as they have found their way really into the head and heart of millions: and so the field-cry "freedom" produced the guillotine, the field-cry "equality" proscriptions, the field-cry "brotherhood" - to name only one example - the entire devastation of the Palatinate, where indeed not only castles and religious institutions, but especially all the property and possessions of the farmers, were obliterated to the last stock, and where the "comrade in command" of those who implored him that the world-betterer should however at least spare their poor cried out, "Everything belongs to us! we leave you only your eyes to cry with!" Thus appeared the common love which unites all the members of the human family! These are the necessary consequences of false ideals! And as little as Frenchmen are naturally morally inferior

---

favorable result of the negotiations" (in Frances Donaldson, *The Marconi Scandal,* London: Rupert Hart-Davis, 1962, p.260f.)]

false ideals

men, so little are the Social Democratic Germans; that they are not they have now taken the opportunity in great measure to demonstrate; they are, however, followers of the fatefully false French ideals and thereby conduce to the downfall of the German state, uninstructed by the so clear language of history and uninstructed - so I hear - by their experience in this bloody war, where they stand in battle against a world of cruelty, dissolution, lies, hate, before enemies who openly express their intention to plunder, to destroy and to make all of Germany into a desert, and where they must however say to themselves that this brutalized world alone has arisen from the influence of the French Revolutionary ideals, which, in the course of a century, has made of valiant men half beasts in envy and baseness of character. One may however hope that this war will contribute to rousing the German working class from the fateful madness into which it has been driven by foreigners and emissaries.

In a moment such as the present I hold it as not only worthy but in the highest degree practical to leave aside the depressions of present day politics and its eternal imperfections in order to come to an understanding of such fundamental questions; for it is these which turn the scale on centuries. Not from the conflict of a chaotic splintering but only from uniformity of morals can a world-conquering Germany arise; and if Germany does not conquer the world (I mean not through violence alone, but through all-round superiority and moral weight), then it would disappear from the map; it is a question of either-or. The England of the rising epoch was fully uniform in its ideals - in spite of the two parties; fully uniform in their ideals are the mutually warring bodies of the present French Chamber: they bicker only about booty; Germany on the other hand is indeed externally united, but inwardly, in the case of all questions concerning politics, uncertain, unclear, restless, excited and distracted. The old ideals do not suffice for it; even the glorious loyalty to the king of the Prussian warrior nobility does not stand in any vital relation to the Germany of Bismarck, and much less do the other particular remains of finer older times. To be sure, the great legacy which the Classicists of thought, of poetry, of political structure and of legal and political scholarship have left behind forms a rich ground on which we stand securely, but they do not give us immediately the political ideals which we need today. We must especially know this, above all, indeed know it inwardly in such a way that we experience it in ourselves and this conviction circulates with the blood in our veins: the Germany which stands before us today is not an old state, but a young state. The roots plunge on all sides into the good, rich, inexhaustibly bestowing antiquity; the people however are newly born and fostered in the sunshine; they are the last of the great peoples;

compared to the young wandering-bird Germany, the United States are a Philistine already become comfort-loving and rather nervous with an anxious bald head and Japan a well conserved tough, overly artful, old man, greedy and avaricious, as old people often are. If it were only its industry, which in the last forty years has multiplied, to me that would not stand for Germany's youth; rather, this is preserved in the growth in all fields; the accomplishments of agriculture -we have seen (p. 55) - have kept pace with those of industry; it is an unheard of joyousness of creativity, of joyousness of work, a time of invention, of experiment, of daring. How much life however lies in the hundred inventions from which the destruction-bringing German submarine arises! Hardly has Germany been cut off from all sources of saltpetre and already it draws the so necessary nitrogen from the wind!

This young people stands now before new tasks. The world situation is an entirely different one from what it was a hundred years before: it is different because Bismarck has built a new Germany - each genius performs more than he himself imagines and knows; it is different because great popular movements have created and prepared for the future surging up new conditions on the surface of our old mother earth, it is however especially different because the relation of man to the Nature mastered by him has been transformed. As regards the popular movements, the situation does not stand favorably for Germany at the moment; here, England and the other English speaking forces have stolen a march on it; in the other respect, on the other hand, Germany is superior to all the peoples of the world: with the scientific age, the age of Germany enters. Yet, only if Germany politically takes up new ideals for guiding principles, not if it - like the majority of its mechanically working and a great part of its bourgeois classes - remains stuck in demonstrably disastrous French false teachings, or if it, like the other classes, contents itself with old traditions and fruitless challenges. Here the Conservative is precisely as limited as the Liberal and Progressive, and Social Democratic as suicidal as the divisions of the Christian religion. Now Germany must begin a state-building politics on the basis of creative ideals, such as correspond to the essential character of the German and to the spirit of our new scientific age. It is not sufficient to deny the formula, "freedom, equality, brotherhood"; for we too want freedom, equality and brotherhood; our reason shows us, however, and we have experienced, besides, that this ideal can serve no political structure as a foundation, but, rather, is obtained only as a result of good politics. Thus has Carlyle, for example (in *Sartor Resartus)* uttered the profound sentence: "Obedience makes one free"[152] and we could add: subordination creates equality and sacrifice forges brotherhood. Still, a political ideal would not be obtained by that. Insofar as the French placed moral demands at the head, they turned the state on its head; that is why it fell. We must go about it differently.

---

152 [Thomas Carlyle, *Sartor Resartus*, Bk.III, Ch.7: "he who is to be my Ruler, whose will is to be higher than my will, was chosen for me in Heaven. Neither except in such Obedience to the Heaven-chosen is Freedom so much as conceivable".]

III

Determination and consequence are the most worthy
of respect in a man. (Goethe)[153]

In the first part of this essay we saw that man - as soon as he wants to perform something great - cannot give up ideals and learnt to respect in the supposed dreamer and enthusiast, who perhaps could not give a full account of his own start, the mediator of heavenly blessing to mankind; in the second part, we experienced the significance of denial as the indispensable preparatory stage for affirmation, a basic truth which is almost always recognized by sober practical men and for which especially Richard Wagner found an exhaustively concise expression: "We may only know what we do not want, then we shall reach, out of involuntary natural necessity, quite certainly that which we want, which will even become clear and conscious to us only then when we have reached it."

From these considerations emerges the special difficulty of the situation for men like us who stand between two epochs. That thorough transformations of the political conditions must take place and happen, that the present situation is untenable because it is unworthy and unreasonable and has not risen to the necessities, that every observing, thinking man knows; yet, the future hovers before our eyes as

---

153 [*Wllhelm Meisters Lehrjahre*, Bk.VI, "Bekenntnisse einer schönen Seele". The full sentence is "So ist Entschiedenheit und Folge nach meiner Meinung das Verehrungswürdigste am Menschen" (Thus, in my opinion, are determination and consequence the most worthy of respect in a man)].

incomprehensible even as, say, the not yet victoriously pervasive agriculture in the imagination of a reflecting hunter of primeval times, since we men are completely incapable of conjuring up artificially in our brain that which has not yet been experienced - even as little as we may invent any animal or plant form which we have not seen; and so we always spring back to the already trusted shore where we at least feel solid ground under our feet, and try to persuade ourselves that it will continue on so. One, however, who agrees to the unrestricted denial - at least, so I believe - finds himself on the way to greater clarity. For, the French Revolutionary idea which surrounds us signifies one of the possible attempts to introduce a political novelty and this attempt must be considered as entirely unsuccessful - theoretically unfortunate and frustrated by history; insofar as we expel this radical attempt as radically from us, there enters a presentiment of better things into our consciousness, whereby I mean: the belief in the possibility, indeed in the certain reality, of a political future better in essential points, suited to the new conditions of life, obtains for us if not exactly a "form," however, in this way, a "body."

One may not complain against me for my very guarded caution of expression; the expression corresponds to the thought: I do not have the slightest aptitude to be a dreamer, thus I do note where the outlines are sharp and correspond to a reality, and do not hold a cloud formation for a mountain. The mistake of all the political Utopias of our time - from Saint-Simon to Marx and his followers - consists in the fact that the individual believes that he can build with his isolated brain, as he would do in the case of an art-work, whereas the great transformations of socialized man - of man "as nature" - are always derived from Nature itself, and that means, today, from a growing number of more or less unconsciously operating men emerging suddenly at all quarters who, following their instincts, finally carry all along with them. I do not wish to tamper with Nature in the bargain. Since the break of the war I have, although I live in quiet retirement, and so am politically without importance, received so many, in part plainly grotesque, plans of world-betterment which I have rejected that I would be frightened of the excessive imaginative power of the Germans, if I did not have to say to myself that all that is "vital power," which will sooner or later benefit this unique people. I however wish to content myself, on the way which that denial of the Revolutionary ideal shows us, with inquiring if already certain guiding principles of the future to be striven for did not offer themselves from it, so that we can portray it indeed not fantastically, but be made capable of welcoming it - the coming gift of "God-Nature" - and, instead of offering opposition to it foolishly and cowardly, of smoothing its way to us with trust.

Even the first and fundamental question receives through this sort of observation an unexpected illumination.

What is the state? The Revolution assumes that the state is founded and built by men. Rousseau titled his masterpiece, *Le Contrat Social,* he therefore set out in all seriousness from the supposition that the state has arisen in the way of a contract, the isolated living men of an earlier time met together and said to one another: Now we wish to build a state and enter into reciprocal duties for this purpose.[154] That is an anthropomorphism that cries out to heaven! Nature teaches us something else. The being "man" without any beginnings of socialization would be the most pathetic animal, the most pitiable beast on earth; apart from his limbs, nothing of that which constitutes the notion "man" would be his own. Man does not make the state, but the state makes the man. Only philistine souls, who have never observed and scrutinized Nature at work would find this sentence preposterous. The socialization of living beings of one race to a common work, under definite division of duties and responsibilities and offices is a widespread invention of Nature, which we meet in the different orders of animals and which leads, for example, in the case of birds and apes, to a most highly developed organization whose secure adaptation of parts seems incomprehensible to us foolish reasonable beings. Excellently perfect state formation we find, as is well known, among the ants. Isolated, the ant cannot live; even if one supplies it with everything that it needs - food and drink and living space - separated from its comrades, it dies after a few hours; the idea of an "ant" includes the relation to a state, and this relation once again signifies the obligation to certain activities which are affiliated to and incorporated in other activities of their common existence; the individual is here nothing, the state everything. Let it be remarked incidentally that, from the restless diligence of these little animals, man obtains the impression that they must be the most fortunate beings on earth. It does not occur to me now to follow the example of my brilliant teacher Carl Vogt and to devise political pamphlets from *Untersuchungen über*

---

154 [See J.J. Rousseau, *Du Contrat Social* (1762), Bk.I, Ch.6, where the basic function of the social contract is expressed as "Trouver une forme d'association qui défende et protège de toute la force commune la personne et les biens de chaque associé, et par laquelle chacun, s'unissant à tous, n'obéisse pourtant qu'à lui-meme et reste aussi libre qu'auparavant". Rousseau adds "Ces clauses, bien entendues, se reduisent toutes à une seule: savoir, l'aliénation totale de chaque associé avec tous ses droits à toute la communauté"].

Tierstaaten;[155] we all hate false analogies today; what, however, I wish
to make clear with this to the innumerable crowd of people blind to
Nature is that the state is an invention of Nature, not an elaboration of
the human brain, and that the man without a state - the man such as the
amiable Elisée Reclus and the severe Prince Krapotkin imagine him[156]
- is generally not a "man," but an animal, for which I suggest the name
Bestia miserrima.[157] That in different ages - indeed, also in the same
age - of the earthly life of the human state, according to the conditions
of existence, according to the temperament of the races, according to
the past of the people, etc., it has taken on very different forms, that
does no damage to the truth of the opinion; man "as freedom" even
takes possession of, everywhere and in all fields, the work of man as
"nature" and refashions it according to his mind - himself and others,
for good and for evil. At the moment I have only one thing in mind: to
communicate the conviction that, in the real, true, eternal sense, the
state first makes man a man. In the scientific book of the Parisian
anthropologist Paul Topinard, *L'Anthroplogie et la science sociale*
(1900),[158] I read towards the end of the section on state formation in the
animal kingdom, "L'intérêt individual reduit à lui-meme ne conduit à
rien de durable," from that which the individual demands for himself
nothing arises which possesses duration. From it arises, therefore,
neither language nor civilisation nor culture, neither speech nor art nor
science nor religion; all these qualities which make life for us men
worth living are bound to the state; if man were not a state-building

State is moment of Nature

155 [Karl Christoph Vogt (1817-95), *Untersuchungen über Tierstaaten,* Frankfurt
am Main: Literarische Anstalt, 1851].
156 [Elisée Reclus (1830-1905), geographer and anarchist, was the author of
various works, including the social geography, *L'Homme et la Terre,* 6 vols., Paris:
Librairie universelle, 1905-08. Reclus' earliest anarchist views are to be found in
his *Développement de la liberté dans le monde,* Montauban, 1851, where he writes,
"Notre destinée est d'arriver à cet état de perfection idéale où les nations n'auront
plus besoin d'être sous tutelle d'un gouvernement ou d'une autre nation; c'est
l'absence de gouvernement, c'est l'anarchie, la plus haute expression de l'ordre".
In 1877 Reclus met and collaborated with the Russian prince Peter Kropotkin, also
a geographer, who, after observing the poverty of the Finnish peasantry in 1871,
gave up his ambition of obtaining the secretaryship of the Imperial Geographical
Society in St. Petersburg, and devoted his life to the anarchist cause].
157 [The most miserable animal].
158 [Paul Topinard, *Science et foi, l'anthropologie et la science sociale,* Paris:
Masson et Cie., 1900].

animal from natural necessity, there would be nothing of all that. And just as man first became a "man" through the state, so also is his further growth to what he is today - or can be and to what he will yet be, fully linked to the existence of the state. Everything which the individual as an individual creates requires not only the protection of an organised whole but it springs from its stimulation, and first obtains significance and measure in its echo. The active self-will of man may hide this fundamental truth, but it cannot remain hidden to the thinker, and it is also proved in this way that a bad state brings forth bad men, a good state good, a foolish one foolish and an intelligent one intelligent.

From hence emerges the pressing consequence that the political fundamental question of the Revolution has been set up falsely; for it had to run not as: What does the individual man have to demand as his right from the state founded by him? but: What does the state, which first makes a man a man, for the sake of its further continuance and prosperity, have to demand of each individual? What does the interest of the state require? In all the phenomena of nature, without exception, the individual possesses no intrinsic value, and even the most outstanding individual deserves in its eyes only so much consideration as his performance obtains a relation to the whole. Nature - and what is this if not God's Will transformed into activity? - does not consider the rights and desires and merits of the individual, rather it looks merely at the prosperity of the whole. From this I infer: what this whole demands will correspond to the truth of Nature and will therefore, quite certainly, also comprehensively condition the right, god-willed - in opposition to the selfishly-desired - advancement of all the individual constituents.

If we now do our utmost to set ourselves in the elevated, strict standpoint of Nature, and ask ourselves then which of all conditions will be the decisive one whereby a human state may operate blessedly, then the answer cannot be doubtful: duration is that characteristic without which the state cannot bring forth anything beneficial. We may set up as an axiom that a state with many faults, but lastingly built, will perform more for the advancement of noble humanity than a carefully conceived state without a guarantee of existence. That follows from the fact that the chief task of the state must manifestly be to perform that which the individual cannot perform. The individual is most bound in respect of time; in relation to the whole, all his activity is only a fragment. If the individual represents the transient, without knowledge of the past, without devotion to the future, then the state represents the interests - or better expressed, the intention, the idea - of Nature, for which past and future form a unity. All becoming and growing demands time; Nature does not count like us, it as little lets time be limited to it as it asks how many millions of individuals will perish through war and pestilence. The efficiency of the state grows therefore in geometric proportion to its duration; each interruption signifies a return into the self-willed, signifies the need to embark once again, from the start, on much that was already achieved strenuously.

The first guiding principle which we discover as doubtlessly given is therefore duration. What duration guarantees the state, that is - even if prejudice, selfishness, the tendency of the times thunder against it - what we have to prefer. The shape of the future we cannot divine, but we know one thing surely; from there comes redemption to us, as in the past, so also in the future.

Incidentally, anyone who speaks of duration says more than it perhaps seems to be at first glance. In order to last, the state must possess, along with power, also wisdom. Bloody tyranny, for example, does not guarantee duration. For man is not an ant; rather, to his state-building instinct another instinct serves as equipoise: the instinct to find his happiness in himself and in the small circle enlivened by his self. This "polarity" lies underneath the incomparable significance of the human race (at least among us white people): if the individual has acquired development under the protection of the state, he will be in difficulty when the armour presses against him; the happiness of the individual forms a living component of the texture of the unsentimental whole. Therefore the most lasting state will grant a maximum of right, of freedom, of leniency. The word "maximum" is naturally to be understood according to the age and race: the arbitrariness of a black chieftain can found, in opposition to the unbridled violent deeds of blood-thirsty wild beasts, a supposedly constitutional state - a maximum. One, therefore, who speaks of a lasting state speaks of - I shall express myself briefly and concisely - a "good" state, of a state in which the benefits of freedom, equality and brotherhood, so foolishly vehemently demanded as "rights," will be present in the highest measure to the practical possibility given at the moment. Goethe makes clear in one of his apparent paradoxes, in reality unfathomably profound observations: "In all 'forms of government', as they are also called, freedom and servitude exist in polarity at the same time." The most lasting state will be that which takes the necessary bitterness of servitude through just distribution and, through "polarity," measures out freedom as wisely. The same is true of all the other "polar" needs of the state and human demands, such as strictness and leniency, strength and flexibility, ranking and independence, literal law and fairness, ordering and composure, etc. Anyone who attributes duration as the highest character of the state includes all that *eo ipso* with it.

Now what does duration guarantee the state? It is helpful now to tear oneself from all of the present and to set oneself such a question purely objectively.

The short-lived man should create and maintain a long-lasting work, he should leave behind his momentary interests so that future generations may grow in security, prosperity and happiness; summarized briefly: man should serve humanity! Anyone who considers the question soberly - and that we wish however as reasonable people - must admit: a definite solution is above all impossible; it would demand more from a man than he can perform; God Himself would then have to take the government in His hands. For this reason does Nature offer here, as also otherwise, so often, in all parts of her universal kingdom, the indirect "means": the individual man follows a limited goal, Nature uses this for an unlimited. It is a question of lengthening the life of a man, or, since that is not possible, of extending the duration of his interests beyond his life. Here originates the political value of the family. The celebrated apostle of the Revolution had depicted to us as the free ideal man the man who does not recognize his own children; the "father" on the contrary has cares for his child and grandchild, and if there is not a state which guarantees his laborious work and his will duration, all love lasts only until the grave. Here originates also the political - and that means the human - value of personal, hereditary possession. That there were times without the notion of "possession" cannot be doubted: but the state at that time must have resembled a kaleidoscope. Through the invention of possession entered the element of continuity; only now can one organise, only now can that spiritual-moral growth arise for which otherwise no point of support is vouchsafed. The Revolutionary ideal thought of it indeed differently; for it taught us through the mouth of its by far most talented, sincere and therefore most sympathetic representative, Pierre Joseph Proudhon: "La proprieté, c'est le vol,"[159] possession is robbery; logically considered, a wonderful performance, for there can be "robbery" only when possession enjoys recognition. If, however, Proudhon's sentence be interpreted as: only the abstract commonality may possess, then it is to be retorted to it: The possession of "all" is not a possession but the lawful prevention of possession, with the consequence that that "instinct" which Schiller pointed to as indispensable does not arise.[160] One does not ignore the essential movements of the human mind without consequences. It may be

---

159 [See P.-J. Proudhon (1809-65), *Qu'est-ce que la proprieté? ou Recherches sur le principe du droit et du gouvernement (1840)*].

160 cf. Chamberlain, *Die Zuversicht*, p. 17.

demonstrated that common possession was always only a stage, a childhood of the state (Schurtz),[161] individual possession signifies a higher state in the development of human values: here as everywhere the Revolutionaries stick to outmoded ideas and recommend regression as progress. Moralists have often pointed to the moral disadvantages and dangers of possession and wealth; possession creates inequality, brings hardships, fosters many degenerate phenomena. To all these complaints it must be retorted that Nature inquires as little after these moral as after the sentimental complaints: what duration grants the state is good, what its duration endangers is bad: the invention of possession therefore signifies an enormous gain, in that it creates men who feel a strong interest in the lasting continuance of the state reaching beyond their life. As regards the disadvantages, it is thus the affair of men "as freedom" to restrain themselves, to stand erect and to bring things to order as far as it will go; thus indeed arises religion, philosophy, culture.

Here, however, it is necessary to differentiate clearly. For, possession undergoes in our century a crisis which leads to phenomena in which it neutralizes itself as it were. Possession (earlier "occupation"),[162] even as the Latin "possessio," signifies first of all "occupying," "domiciling," "settling"; possession, in the genuine and characteristic sense, is the appropriation of land and ground, of "immobile property"; only mother earth does not forget - at least not in the aeons which come into the view of mankind - and therefore holds on to a notion of a not transient "possession"; no other possession guarantees duration. That it, as a born wanderer, obtain a footing, that it strike roots in a definite piece of the earth, that it settle and possess: that is for the state decisive. The persisting cultivation of the soil, where each generation inherits from the past generations and stores up for the coming generations: that is the prototype of every constructive cultural activity. "The state and the soil belong necessarily together," says Friedrich Ratzel.[163] That also moveable goods must be estimated as "possession" is from the standpoint of the state a necessary consequence, but of far less significance; for the source of every

---

161 [See footnote 135 above.]

162 [The German words referred to here are 'Besitz' and 'Besetz'].

163 [Friedrich Ratzel, *Politische Geographie*, München: R. Oldenbourg, 1897, p.4: "When we speak of a state, we mean, exactly as in the case of a city or a road, always a piece of humanity and a human work and, at the same time, a part of the soil."].

property - even to the "wandering" - lies in the soil which, year in year out, stores up the gifts of the sun - which is the same as that wherever a living animal is caged or captured, where coal is demanded or granite broken, as wherever corn, clover, vegetables, fruits, wood, etc. grow: all that is traced back to the power of the sun. One may consider mobile property as lent by the immobile; it is a derivative possession; whoever follows things sufficiently far, from one cause to the other, will find that confirmed everywhere: true property leads at the end of the zig-zag course, today often extremely complicated, back to the sun-warmed earth; one who possesses this is the true "possessor"; the true possessors build the foundations of the state. In the course of the last century, however, a development has occurred due to which a fiction - which has existed already from unthinkable times in one form or other - money - naturally only a sign, a symbol for a possession lying somewhere - has surpassed possession itself, so that now the true possession is forced to the background through an apparent possession. A man who possesses only a writing table and a safe can today be richer than the greatest possessor of land in the world; indeed he "occupies" nothing, but he is rich, and that implies, according to the wisdom of speech, that he is a king. That here a danger to the state as a lasting institution is threatened cannot be doubted. This man has no land, therefore also no fatherland. To him peace is as dear as war; and since its growth is not conditioned by the sun and work, but by increased restlessness, by a rushing to and fro whereby something clings to his hand at all times, he loves unrest, change, catastrophes of every sort. He subjugates the state; he destroys the individual which the state out of its own interest protects and raises. For that reason I believe I glimpse even here a guiding principle of the future: the state must check this evil. How should it be able to do that? I have said: I am not a prophet, I build no castles in the wind: I would like only to point out directions to the expectant gaze, from which redemption will certainly come, that we may be prepared to perceive and recognise it when the ripeness of the times leads it in. Here something radical will happen, otherwise the Revolutionary ideal will triumph - which swims in gold - and, with it, chaos and barbarism. There are different plans to abolish gold entirely, to let it, as in old fairy-tale times, serve more as ornament only: they give me the impression of fantastic Utopias; perhaps I am the fool and Mr. Silvio Gesell[164] and his consorts are the wise men; I would be

---

164 [Silvio Gesell (1862-1930) was an economist who became the first Finance Minister of the Bavarian Soviet Republic. Gesell's chief work was *Die natürliche*

happy to be able to believe that. But why should not the state, just as it arrested and politically organised troops - earlier scattered in a thousand hands - turning curses into blessings, one day seize all the financial businesses of the entire land, pay off the erstwhile possessors appropriately modestly and from now on lead the entire gold business as an exclusive monopoly itself? The indispensable intermediary, the entire elastic machinery without which agriculture, industry, trade would be subjected to inflexible obstacles, would continue to exist thereafter as before, the savings of the individual would be just as well managed as today; we see it indeed in the savings banks and in the trade in postal cheques; however, the billions which have been made out of this without any real work, would henceforth flow into the state, thus to the public, reducing the burden of taxes; and what is the main thing: we would be saved from the greatest international - and that means "state destroying" - danger. For through this the means would be placed in our hands to control the terrible situation of billions and monopolies. In it, the individual sets himself up against the state; as, earlier, the crude savage with clubs and arrows against the ploughing farmer, so also this new, more cowardly, man of violence against all honest work. I recommend to everybody to read Wells' book on the United States.[165] Wells, the English socialist, swears on the Revolutionary ideal; but how he is frightened by what he discovers in America, the land of democratic freedom, where six year-old boys perform twelve hours of factory work![166] The billionaire rules there without any limitations, corrupt elective bodies, corrupt administration, corrupt justice. Whether the billionaire bribes or whether he builds philanthropic foundations: he causes calamity everywhere. How the foolish world celebrates Carnegie!; now we learn that he, through his foundations for professors and students, binds the universities to himself, and has obliged them to certain teachings, so, for example, to the adoration of England and to the persecution of Germany. Thus does the freedom of

---

Wirtschaftsordnung durch Freiland undFreigold, 1916, which attacked the gold standard and suggested radical currency reform.]

165 [H.G. Wells, The Future in America: A search after realities, London: Chapman and
Hale Ltd., 1906].

166 [Wells, op.cit., Ch. VI, where he points to the abomination of child employment as "another aspect of that great theory of the liberty of property and the subordination of the state to business, upon which American institutions are based."].

science appear where the criminal self-will of the individual forces its way on it.

All these things are only fleeting suggestions: perhaps they may provoke to thoughts of the "holiness" of possession and of the "evil" of possession. I mean that, as soon as we, instead of applying arguments of moral indignation or of ranting politically, set ourselves in a sober standpoint: what benefits the state? what harms the state? we see significantly more clearly; thereby is much obtained.

From this same standpoint I would like to cast a glance at the constitutional question, insofar as it accords decisive significance to a parliament elected by the general public.

The whole world has, in this connection, sunk today to a slave of the Revolutionary ideal; and yet this ideal is, before which all with exception, on this point, bow to the ground, here too so basically false, so incredibly foolish, that future generations will not comprehend how it was possible to stultify even the intelligent among us so long. Herbert Spencer, the English thinker, in a political religious context an unlimited freethinking spirit, judged at the end of his life: "The disastrous superstition of our present is the madness of the divine right of parliamentary representation."[167] It is however obvious that the 'demos', the people, could actually rule only in very small states, as in Athens and in early Rome. Aristotle teaches: a state cannot include 100,000 men and still be called a "state."[168] But everybody knows what even there the 'demos' has accomplished: all the greatness of Athens - political, scientific, artistic - was achieved under the demanding rule of individuals, all narrowmindedness, all error, the rapid downfall of the state, is the work of the people, who were called, out of well-minded foolish idealism, to cooperation and decision in questions for which they possessed no aptitude nor ever will. Anyone who wishes to learn more accurately on this should reach out for Julius Schvarcz's multi-volume *Die Demokratie* (1898),[169] or Croiset's *Les Democraties*

---

167 [Herbert Spencer, *The Man versus the State,* London: Williams and Norgate, 1910 Ch.IV: "The great political superstition of the past was the divine right of kings. The political superstition of the present is the divine right of parliaments — However irrational we may think the earlier of these beliefs, we must admit that it was more consistent than is the latter" (p.78)].

168 [Aristotle, *Ethica Nichomachea,* 1170b31: "Ten people would not make a city, and with a hundred thousand it is a city no longer" (tr. H. Rackham)].

169 [Julius Schvarz, *Die Demokratie von Athen,* Leipzig: E. Avenarius, 1901].

antiques. [170] To this another decisively important consideration presents itself: In Athens as in ancient Rome, and as still today in the plebiscite of Switzerland, the people share *in corpore* in the political transactions; that is, in most states, impossible; and so arose the modern invention of the so-called parliamentary representation, of which fortunate antiquity knew nothing. The "ruling" people is with us not the people, but a group of gentlemen X, Y and Z, who are elected by the "people" as their representatives. Now, to be sure, it may be imagined that in many questions directly concerning their existence, the people in its entirety may possess a - even if not a far-sighted and finely considered - yet expert, clever judgement; the agreement of an entire people, man for man, in a question which concerns everyone and which everyone understands, will often turn out even as overwhelmingly right as the quiet agreement of the German people in the war which surrounds us. That, however, the general mass should be capable of that most difficult work - of the estimation of the character and the talent and the power of judgement of individual men, of the fine comparative psychology which the election of a "representative" requires - is a plainly monstrous supposition. Thus democracy necessarily leads to demagogy; the two words are in practice interchangeable. It may be reckoned in advance, with scientific definiteness, that in universal franchise, for one expert and inwardly upright friend of the fatherland, five babblers and as many business politicians will be voted. Already the fact that votes must be won through speeches signifies a suspicious aberration of judgement. Swift[171] - one of the most acute of men - establishes on the ground of life-long observation that - apart from isolated intelligent talents - the so-called gift of speech always implies a narrow circle of ideas, matched by a poverty of vocabulary. These are the people who now populate our Parliament! Science knows of a "selection of the fittest"; we practise the selection of the narrow-minded and the shallow-speaking. While precisely the fittest men of all of the entire people - the wisest and the strongest, for that reason also, often, the most silent - would be good enough to steer the ship of the state, we search out the chatterboxes for it. The word "Parlia-ment" signifies in German, "gossip shack." If it were possible to collect the quantity of energy which is yearly lost in our part of the earth in political speeches, it would suffice to keep the entire electric network of Europe going for a long time. And these parliamentary

---

170 [Alfred Croiset, *Les démocraties antiques,* Paris: E. Flammarion, 1909].

171 [Jonathan Swift (1667-1745), the Irish satirical novelist].

effusions lasting for hours operate devastatingly on broad sections of the population, for they are registered in shorthand, as if the gods were speaking, and printed, as if they were worth reading; and now sit thousands, whose further development of the understanding and elevation of the soul is so necessary, and lose every free hour on this empty reading material.

Thereby, however, is not enough, by far, said of our parliamentarism; rather, further things come into consideration which work more threateningly. If need be, one could think of a very cultured people - let us say the future German - that it at one time would come about that it would not let itself be led by the nose through words and programs, but it would for the most part elect really efficient representatives devoted to the welfare of the state. That happens - as the farmer says - in the week with four Sundays; still, however, let us imagine it. We can do so much more easily since the different German "things" or assemblies of the present are thankfully not fully, by a long shot, democratized yet, even as little as the French Chamber was fifty years ago, and in consequence of which they exhibit a noteworthy amount of talent and goodwill. Two unsurpassable things cling nevertheless to every parliamentary government, and even if it were constituted of a selection of the people: the majority and mass-psychology.

I would like every German to be obliged by law to learn by heart Goethe's immortal judgement: "Nothing is more repulsive than the majority ...": there I must stop to underline the sentence: Nothing is more repulsive than the majority! Yes, nothing! Next to the tyranny of a chamber majority, Genghis Khan is to me an angel of God; for - as the same thinker says in another place - despotism has at least this for itself that it calls forth "great character," whereas the majority constituted of several hundred invulnerable and irresponsible speech-giving- and parliamentary allowance-swallowing individuals, represents the stupid might of the mass - "might" is a fine word: the majority are the grains of sand of the desert which bury up the cultural work of thousands of years. Still, let us return to Goethe: "Nothing is more repulsive than the majority; for it consists of a few powerful leaders, of rascals who accommodate themselves, of weak people who assimilate themselves, and of the mass which toddles along after without knowing in the least what it wants." Where, in the entire history of the world, has one seen that the better judgement, the wiser prudence is to be found among the majority? This political system held by all men today as an indisputable dogma I consider to be the crudest solution that ever was sought of an advanced, difficult problem: in the case of every other form of government, at least there is the possibility, if not indeed the likelihood, that it will often govern cleverly and on occasion excellently; in the case of the system of universal suffrage with parliamentary majority decisions, it is mathematically certain that it will always govern precisely so badly as it is possible to do, if the entire state machine is not dispersed. What is the glorification of Schiller worth, if we do not listen to the great man's words:

> One should weigh the votes and not count them,
> The state must fall sooner or later,
> Where the majority triumphs and unreason decides.[172]

In Germany one does not note that with complete clarity, since the Council of Ministers[173] and the Chancellor of the Reich, responsible only to the Kaiser, work in unceasing battle against it; that was indeed the case already in the old Federal Imperial Parliament,[174] otherwise there would have for long been no more Germany; and even so has everything great which has made Germany what it is today, from the year 1870, been won in a battle against parliamentary representation. Even in England a great tradition, and especially the dictatorial power of the secret committee of the small ruling group, holds off the catastrophe. Otherwise, however, one needs only to look around oneself to see where we will reach on this path and to ask oneself sorrowfully what devilish spirit holds a bandage before one's eyes that one blindly runs into destruction. One thunders against the affectation of foreign things and holds it as a betrayal of the fatherland when men have their trousers sent from London and women their hats from Paris: the most destructive affectation of things foreign is, however, the belief in the unassailable value and the decisive significance of parliamentary representation derived from universal suffrage: for this reason will Germany still be destroyed if a complete transformation of public opinion does not take place soon.

I must bring forward yet another observation - on the influence of mass psychology - the most important of all, which is related to every parliamentary government, no matter whether it arises from the universal suffrage or from something else: it has already often become

---

172 [Schiller, *Demetrius* (Fragment), Act 1.11. 475 ff. The preceding lines are equally apt here: "What is the majority? The majority is nonsense,/ Understanding has always been only among the few"].

173 [Bundestag].

174 [Bundesreichstag].

audible in one form or other, yet men are occasionally overcome by deafness as by blindness. The already often mentioned Gustave le Bon was astonished, when he, for the first time, studied the history of the French Revolution carefully, at the discovery that the members of the different Revolutionary parliaments always voted differently from what they had promised, and so took decisions from stage to stage which contradicted their convictions. "Les assemblées révolutionaires votaient sans cesse des mesures contraires aux opinions de chacun de leurs membres."[175] Sometimes, to be sure, they did what they did not want to do, what they had expressly held to be bad and disastrous, simply from cowardice, since the people flocked outside; yet, that did not hold true absolutely in all cases; always there is a remarkable distance between the written and spoken utterances of the members and that to which these same members then let themselves be swept away in their common deliberation. Le Bon reaches the conviction that that which he investigated in another well known work as mass-soul *(Psychologie des foules)*[176] is at work in all such conferences, and that means: reduction of the sobriety of the individual, rise of his passion, the hypnotic influence and, in consequence of that, preponderance of the brutal nature of the will over and above the more finely organised brain. Parliaments like the old English, like the earlier États généraux in France, as still today in the Prussian State Parliament, do not allow these facts to emerge so clearly to the surface, on the one side because very strong interests are represented, because - if I may express myself thus - things, facts, relations are represented more than parties and opinions, on the other side because its sphere of influence is limited; however, the more "absolute" the Parliament becomes, partly through the universality of the suffrage (a situation which, as is well known, has not yet been reached in England at the moment), partly through the widening of powers, partly through the election of completely dislocated representatives (as attorneys or professional politicians, who originate neither in landed property nor in any trade or manual labor), the more strongly does this psychological law emerge: it is a natural law and, for that reason, cannot in any way be evaded. If we lock up

---

175 [Gustave le Bon, *La Révolution Française et la psychologie des révolutions,* Paris; E. Flammarion, 1912, Première Partie, Livre II, Ch.5, Sec.l: "La majorité des membres de la Convention édicta les mesures les plus contraires à ses opinions, sous l'influence d'un très petit nombre de semblables meneurs"].
176 [This was the subject of his study *La Psychologie des foules,* Paris: F. Alcan, 1895].

four hundred fit men in a room with the task of granting money, of deliberating laws, of judging foreign politics, etc., then scientific observation allows us to predict with unfailing certainty: the average judgement of this four hundred will be significantly reduced and the tendency to imprudence increased; besides, the less noble elements - the less free-thinking, the less fine-feeling - will get the upper hand. Anyone who looked diligently would bring forth proof from all quarters. I chanced on something most valuable not long ago in a letter of Bismarck's to Motley,[177] from the year 1863; he speaks of the Prussian Representative House and calls the members at first simply "foolish"; immediately, however, he takes back this word that escaped from him in a moment of passion: "Foolish in its generality is not the right expression; the people are, considered individually, partly properly prudent, for the most part educated, of correctly German university culture," and so he arrives at the view: "They become childish as soon as they meet *in corpore;* as a mass foolish, as individuals reasonable."[178] The German statesman thus judges without a preconceived theory, from practical experience, literally exactly as the French psychologist from his study of history.[179] I call upon yet another 'king's evidence' to hear once again a judgement from another human point of view. Honoré de Balzac, the mighty poet-visionary whose significance achieves increasing recognition the more numbers of his contemporaries sink into the cloud of forgetfulness, writes (in *Les Paysans)*[180] of the French Chamber of his time: "Neuf cents intelligences, si grandes qu'elles puissent etre, se rapetissent en se faisant foule"; the understanding power of nine hundred men who, taken singly, may be of greater significance, shrink together as soon as they sit united in a mass conference.

---

177 [John Lothrop Motley (1814-77), American historian and diplomat, noted for his histories of the Netherlands].

178 [See letter dated April 17,1863, from Prince Otto von Bismarck to John Motley, in *The Correspondence of John Lothrop Motley,* ed. G.W. Curtis, London, J. Murray, 1889, Vol.11, p.126f.].

179 Bismarck might have recalled Schiller's diptych against the "learned society": Everybody, if one consider him singly, is reasonably clever and understanding; If they are *in corpore,* they immediately become a fool.
[See P. Schiller, 'Votivtafeln', Nr.50 (in the *Nationalausgabe,* Band II, Teil 1)].

180 [Honoré de Balzac (1799-1850), the novelist, was a monarchist and Catholic who feared the impending anarchy of the class warfare. The first part of his *Les Paysans* was published in 1844, and the entire work posthumously in 1855].

No man in the world is capable of gainsaying this fact; eternal natural laws do not cease to operate because one disregards or despises or scorns them. Besides, however, the parliamentary form of government - insofar as a Parliament arisen from universal suffrage should form the decisive political power in a country - is judged once and for all. All that we get to hear about them is rhetoric. This way cannot possibly be the way of the future; we must accustom ourselves to consider the abolition of this legacy of the French Revolution as inevitable and to look in other directions. Luther once spoke the words: "To government belong not base, bad people, nor knaves, but heroes, understanding, wise and spirited people in whom one may confide trust"; how we should arrive at this hero is a not easily answerable question, at any rate the Revolutionary ideal does not show us the way to it.

From these various negations already begins to arise - as the wise have predicted - something political: the estimation of the state as a state which it cannot be wise to cripple, the estimation of durability as the criterion in all political questions, the estimation of possession as the foundation of the state, which we may not allow to be disintegrated into either communism or false values, because both shake the state, the certainty that in parliamentary representation in its present form there lies not the promised salvation, but indeed evil.

In the hope of grasping something more precise, we wish in the fourth section of this hitherto generally conducted observation to go over to the problem in so far as it concerns Germany.

IV

Here I behold the stout and manly prowess
of the Germans, disdaining servitude.
Milton[181]

It is always best to grab the bull by the horns; if one does not succeed in throwing the animal that has become wild to the ground, then one throws oneself on its back and rides it to exhaustion; whereas the coward is simply skewered. I have met not a few men who know quite precisely what misery the Imperial Parliament has already suffered and also how unpromising it is on the basis of this conception to hope for a great future for Germany; they are inconsolable about it, let their head hang and sigh: "There is no salvation; the universal and at the same time secret suffrage is already here; the German does not want to be settled worse than the citizens of other nations; it can never be possible to set the political clock backwards, etc., etc." This wisdom I hold to be folly. Who is this "German"? and who knows what the German wants? In the main question, in the case of such complaints, the parties of the Socialists come to the mind; like the other political "parties," this is also an artificially arisen one, become important through influences from outside, not a German phenomenon based in the soil. Anyone who was unbelieving until now needs only to observe the present war: this splendid soldier will be ready every day - indeed, happy and more than happy - instead of complaining and worrying year in year out, instead of preaching the nonsense of a class-war, instead of

---

181 [John Milton, *Second Defense of the People of England against the infamous libel entitled The Cry of the Royal Blood to Heaven, against the English parricides*].

saying "no" to everything and thereby taking no part in the building-up of the state, as hitherto; he will, I say, be happy, as outside there, so also inside within the Reich, to work together, to operate together, to build together, each in his place. One sees it already in many organisations, so long as political zealots do not interfere with them, or where they have been thrown out because practical workers wished to demand practical goals rather than programme phrases. Thus, for example, already "in a great number of (German) cities there are not generally (political) factions present within the assembly of city commissioners"; and even in those cities where there are political factions in the city administrative bodies, "experience teaches that the important communal decisions are taken without essential connection with the political party programme." [182] Thus that complaint - the German "wants" [183] - makes no impression on me. The matter lies otherwise: I shall never believe that the German worker is won over by the French Revolutionary ideal; in it he deceives himself and we deceive ourselves; he, however, does not want things to remain in such a way as they stand at the moment, and therein he is right. The power of German Socialism does not lie in its programme forced on it from outside, not in its despotic leadership, not in the instigatory activity of its press organs; all that will disappear overnight as if it had never been; this power arises from the fact that millions of men have ideals - for that always provides the highest human power. We have seen that such political ideals arising from man "as nature" never possess in advance a firm shape: joined to a negation of that which it does not want is a merely cloudy representation of what it wants; the original corn cultivator did not want any longer to restlessly range over the eternally alien earth, in hunting and plundering and cannibalistic murder- and robbery-raids, and he dreamed of another, better future, apparently very absurdly and fantastically impossible: from his dreams arose the foundations of the great human culture whose possibility he could have had no idea of. A similar power circulates, in my opinion, in our present, and I find it natural that it stirs most forcefully above all in those classes which are burdened the least with historic ballast and inherited formalism. In spite of many bad incidental occurrences, I cherish a strong trust in the German "working class" - as the foolish term runs, as if scholars, officials, military officers, businessmen, lords of houses, etc. did not work; there is present there much talent, much will, perhaps also

---

182 cf. Councillor Dr. Hans Luther, "Das deutsche Staatsbürgertum und seine Leistungen in der Selbstverwaltung" in *Deutschland und der Weltkrieg* [ed. 0. Hintze, P. Meinecke, H. Oncken, H. Schumacher] (Teubner, 1915), p.227.
183 [Chamberlain is referring to the sentence on the preceding page.]

creative ability, more at any rate than among the fundamental enemies. In reality, however, this power stirs in men of all circles, and we lack now only the simplicity and that "prowess" which the great Milton admired in the Germans, that is, an unquestionably frank fearlessness which allows a man to acknowledge with guiltless uprightness what he holds inwardly to be true - acknowledge in word and deed. Belief in God - I find no other word for the natural disposition - is indispensable in all decisive activity; but we are so entangled in the folds of the culture hanging around us, so anguished by the thousand threatening gestures of the past catastrophes, so twisted in basic slogans and articles of belief, in viewpoints and considerations and leniencies, that it is difficult for us to throw ourselves naked into the arms of God-Nature, certain that He and that She - the Mind and the Phenomenon - will bear us in sheltering hands to the opposite shore that is our destination. "One cannot set back the political clock," do you say? Indeed, who then will set it back? But only the Revolutionary! Anyone who reads the "Convention" finds it filled with Latin and Greek names of heroes; a gigantic reaction presents itself to the mind of those undiscerning enthusiasts: the return to the form of government of the Hellenic *demos* and to ancient Roman *res publica*. That in the one case slave-economy, in the other case the iron-hard and inviolably sacred structure of the family unit dispensed with the conditioning possibility for democracy - that was not taken into consideration; of equality the Hellene as a born aristocrat knew nothing; the Roman, an uncouth farmer who rose entirely in the service of the state, nothing of personal freedom - that remained unobserved; it was a self-intoxication on false representations and empty words. In general, there has been no more reactionary politics on earth than Communism: it sets man back to prehistoric times; to this extent is Rousseau, judged by himself the most upright, however the most discerning of this school because he admits it expressly and recognizes the destruction of all civilisation and all culture as the precondition of it. What the Revolution has produced is violent reaction; Germany's way leads in the exactly opposite direction, and every political form forced on it from the Revolution forms a brake - we have experienced that in the last forty five years sufficiently[184] - and falsifies the entire political life of the nation. Germany does not do well to borrow from France and England; these directions are not auspicious to it at all; it should have the courage to confront its own ideals, to preserve everything which the future demands which is worth preserving and to create everything anew from necessity.

---

184 [Chamberlain is referring to the final unification of Germany in 1870 after the war against Napoleon III].

Now how will these German political ideals be created? I pose this question, and I answer it in the sense of the previous sections: it is not my intention to deal with fantastic plans, whose fruitlessness would be associated with the self-will of all; I imagine the transformation which we confront much too deeply penetrating for a so-called "politician" to be able to accomplish it from his limited viewpoint; that is a work for man "as nature," i.e. for a public operating thousandfold - like a natural power - I seek only to contemplate precisely some chief guiding principles: through denial and accord, however, one steps out of the most desperate cloud and obtains thereby an ability to glimpse the future clearly - or at least somewhat less indistinctly. The neglect of the practicians does not destroy my equanimity: if things went according to brains of this calibre, we men would still today be tearing raw flesh with our teeth and would have neither bread nor wine. We do better to ask Nature which leads and rules us men as well as her other creations.

An important first question She answers with all clarity: where Nature - as Nature - creates states, there also does She create monarchy and unequal ranks. The real natural basis of this procedure is that it is possible only in this way to create a true organism -expressed in German: a homogeneous form constituted of parts which belong to one another and to the whole. If the parts are all equal to one another, then no form arises, only mass, and therefore also no unity, no ordered giving and taking, no life; in the entire realm of Nature the law is valid: the more different the parts, the higher is the whole. Already this consideration should suffice to convince everyone capable of thought that the republican and indeed the communistic form of the state stands low in the series of possibilities and promises neither duration nor a rich life. However, the events of the last century must have taught with overwhelming clarity anyone who is less accessible to the compelling instruction that is to be obtained from thoughtful natural observation. For, always, as soon as a great country goes over to the republican constitution, it does not enjoy a peaceful day any more. Even the United States finds itself in reality in a condition of unbroken anarchy and criminal self-will: only the despotic might of the President in power and of the incredibly complicated political machinery prevents destruction like a dam from inside, yet in such a way that the strength of the state is almost entirely consumed by this mechanical activity of resistance and must remain beggarly poor in constructive activity. In France, the citizens believed in aiming for freedom, equality, and brotherhood, and they have reached a shameless plutocracy which systematically deceives the people, which shrinks hardly more from any crime and is so incapable of protecting the personal security of the citizen that today, in Paris, one must go out in the evening with a loaded revolver, as if one lived among savages. Italy - a republic with a mock kingdom - perhaps stands closer to full hopeless anarchy: the rulers are men without honour and conscience, cowardly and tyrannical demagogues as well, gossips who are out only to fill their purse with gold, come whatever will or may later; a government which assigns a professional criminal like Mr. Rappaport d'Annunzio for the stultification of the people has reached a degree of moral depravity which even a few years ago would have been impossible. These are already South American conditions! The republics of Central and South America live, as is well known, in chronic anarchy, one revolution follows another, often many hostile presidents rule at the same time ... God knows, the man must be blind who is not instructed and converted by so many facts, who still hopes something from the Revolutionary ideal and does not understand that even the worst monarchy offers more guarantee of duration, of freedom, of human activity and human values.

The king however must be a king. If the state bears as its highest point a deception - the alleged highest leader a theatrical king with a paper crown on his head, behind whom hide the true wire-pullers - then not much is obtained: Nature expects from a moral being truth, not appearance; therefore are they moral, thinking, not merely blindly acting, beings. I recall Paul Verlaine's verses written in memory of Ludwig II of Bavaria:

> Vous fûtes un poete, un soldat, le seul Roi
> De ce siècle où les rois se font si peu de chose![185]

So it is! To kingship belongs poetry. Everything great that man creates on earth springs up from his imagination, and even as foolish as children brought up without fairy tales become through experience, so foolish a thing also arises when grown-up men do not wish to understand that the worth of the "king" lies precisely herein that we - owing to our human imaginative power - choose a man and endow him with the characteristics and attributes and rights of a highest entity. In him we reveal how highly we know to value the state. He disappears entirely from our view as a limited personality - or, if he is incidentally significant as a man, then we know to separate this in our mind from the bearer of the crown; as a king he is entirely idea and entirely duty. In the great heroic poem of the Indian Aryans[186] it is called: "The fathers had both worlds (that is the fate of men here and in the other world) in view

---

185 ['La mort de S.M. le Roi Louis II de Bavière', *La Revue wagnérienne*, July 1886].
186 The *Mahabharata*.

when they created the king, the exceedingly great being, in that they thought that he would be the embodied Law." The more highly and more strictly we form our ideal of kingship, so much more unavoidably does the king find himself forced into the destined path. To believe that a king could "reign and at the same time enjoy" is termed by Goethe's Faust "a great mistake." In him the idea of the state becomes visible as it were, therefore the idea of universal duty, of subordination - at all levels - under the welfare of the whole; that is what is expressed in kingship: the subordination of the individual to the whole. This idea - not its incidental bearer - is worth our reverence; the more unconditional the devotion to this idea, the more unshakable the state. Paul de Lagarde, the great German scholar, utters profound words in that he indicates that a genuine kingship demands a "kingly people": in a true organism every part even bears a conditioning-conditioned relationship to all the others; giving is a taking, taking a giving. The reverence paid to the king as the bearer of the idea of the state radiates back to those who give evidence of reverence: the entire state is elevated. In contrast to which it is very striking how the general feeling of respect between man and man - indeed, even the self-respect of the individual - generally sinks, as soon as there is not the one in whom we blend, as in a focal point, all reverence together, which, broken thousand-fold, ennobles the unnumbered relationships within the state and - as our ancestors would have said - humanises them. In and for itself the regiment of Napoleon III was not especially noble; how differently however was the entire public life of France formed then from today! how much more decency and consideration and concession! Frightful brutalisation has gripped all circles and finds its corresponding expression in the press. On such - sometimes at first hardly noticeable - things, on such hovering voices, depends enormously much; they model the mind from childhood on in a certain form; in the revolutionary state already every beardless youth stands with self-conscious insolence: I demand my rights, I will only obey when it suits me; in the genuinely monarchic state, the young man enters life with the attitude: my first duty is to pay heed to the rights of others recognised by the state, through obedience will I earn rights and freedom. Such facts possess the unshakability of mountains, because they arise from the given nature of men: on the one side arise state-destroying, on the other state-maintaining powers. The guiding principle of the future for Germany points to monarchy: for it requires for its task the highest measure of strength and the least measure of inner dissension; it requires also the greatest number of capable, pure, unselfish men in all leading positions, and that can - as we have already seen in the previous sections - never be expected of a parliamentary government, which prefers the mediocre with mathematical necessity and almost always falls prey finally to the ignoble. Anyone who speaks of a republic in Germany belongs to the gallows. The monarchical ideal is here the sacred law of the land.

Monarchy represents an age-old German heritage; on the other hand, a second political principle of the German future - insofar as it is already felt to be rising all around us, though unconsciously - would be new: the guiding principle doubtlessly pointed out to it of a scientific organisation of the entire political life. The fact that it is capable of it is the trump-card which Germany holds in its hand, the only one; if it knows how to play it, then it can become the decisive power among all the peoples of the world. This second guiding principle stands in strict harmony with the first: organisation and kingship point to each other. Now one may complain: each state is an organisation, the German Reich is that to a high degree and what a wonderful work of organisation is the world-empire of Great Britain, under whose authority about 450 million men live![187] I however mean it otherwise; for I say "scientific organisation" and stress thereby the word 'scientific' which for us Germans conjures trusted and therefore easily understandable notions, as, in it, there is elimination of chance and of plain opportunity, the introduction - as decisive - of painfully precise expert knowledge, that means thus true knowledge, not mere supposition and opinion; by "scientific organisation" I understand the same consideration of scientific principles, as have already led in Germany, in the fields of technology, of research, often also of the administration, to unexampled results; of the other [fields] I mention as an example the most painstaking precision in the adaptation of the means at hand to the goal to be achieved, as well as the application of energy in such a way that from a minimum of expense a maximum of performance maybe attained; besides, the division of labor so that every one performs that which he understands and for which he possesses an inclination according to his talents, - that however requires practical systematisation, that means thus, it considers the interconnection of all the parts of every mechanism, etc., etc.

The mastery of nature has become possible only through precise "scientific" observation; and what we call "mastery" is not an arbitrary and unlimited mastery, rather a clever utilisation of the powers at hand, and for the most part earlier hidden, in that we men accommodate ourselves to it and lead it - according to the naturally given possibilities

---

187 To anyone who has no appreciation of this, I recommend a brief, comprehensive work published anonymously by Macmillan in London, 1912, *An analysis of the system of government throughout the British Empire.*

- to that which is useful and required for our goal. In this way are obtained the results which the external conditions of life have fully transformed within a century. The German learned professional has already for a long time been observing the state in a similar way as well as the entire economic machinery within the state: the day thus approaches in which we may abandon the chaotic fortuitousness and haphazardness of the politics until now and organise the state scientifically and rule scientifically - instead of politically. One speaks much in Germany of "dilettantism," and one scolds and complains about it, even where it is not present, and glorifies therefore the professional without observing that one indeed often practices the most inveterate dilettantism oneself; nowhere at all, however, rules more thorough dilettantism so unrestrictedly as in the field of politics! The entire politics hitherto is generally a dilettantism! Not only do we drag with us outdated, inappropriate administrative customs - that would be still the lesser evil; but is it not hair-raising dilettantism when neighbor A and lawyer B and mayor C, who are entirely without military and colonial specialised knowledge, decide how many mountain batteries the German army should include and whether in an African colony a pressingly urgent railway may be built or not? And it is dilettantism to the thousandth power that these men A, B and C obtain this power, decisive for the life of the entire nation, through outstanding talent and demonstrable performances, simply through the vote ballot of 20000 men, of whom at least 12 enjoy only elementary school education and a further 3000 only higher elementary school education, so that for their decision at election of a representative the criterion is certainly not the great standpoint of national politics but - as it is not to be other expected - the more narrowly defined circles of interest familiar to them. How is it possible to allow decisive influence to a counselling body arisen in this way? At any rate this procedure is the opposite of "scientific" and represents a triumph of defective reason. And if we consider that countries like England, France, Italy - generally, all the countries of the Revolutionary ideal - approach a rule by violence, in which, if clever men snatch it, great accomplishments are possible, then we must apprehend: in this way will Germany not only not obtain a predominant position, but it will quite certainly be subjugated and indeed soon. The times are no longer suited to political dilettantism! But, besides, - and above all - Germany wants to foster a noble, free, people worthy of a higher fate. For these different reasons is scientific organisation of the state machine without doubt the first guiding principle of the coming political development: this necessity must be understood and the consequences drawn from the understanding; the next step then manifests itself.

Here it is of the greatest value that England stands before us as a convenient, since isolated, example: an example of what Germany neither can nor should want. To deny the significance of the accomplishment lying before us would be childish; the greatest kingdom by far that the history of the world can record has been erected, maintained and ruled through energy, courage, recklessness (including deception and cruelty), but also through great statesmanship, knowledge of human nature, in general flexibility and adaptability. England is the first - and upto now the only - state to which one may attribute planetary significance; it has been able not merely to subjugate and to rule, but it has been able to extend itself in all parts of the world, with its language and its manners, and so covered our good earth with a web under which, if England now travels further on the way of brutalisation and, nevertheless, maintains power, we all will suffocate. At the moment I speak only of organisation, and my goal is to make clear that the organisation of the British world empire, even if it be also masterly and the wide extension indicate masterly characteristics in this people, is not scientific but the opposite. England has fostered strong, fearless, clever men in thousands, who - be it in the state service, be it on their own – already in their youth fly into the wide world; if they deal on their own, no initiative is too bold for them, if they deal for the state, then they bear without hesitation the hardest responsibility; if one wishes to summarize developed relations in a single sentence: England rules through strength of character. On the other hand, the German – to be sure, with regard to its state, still a little chaotic - in research and industry, in technology, recently also in finance, as well as in many of the so-called organisations related to autonomous administration and, besides, in increasing measure, in his entire thought and action, proceeds scientifically, for which he manifestly possesses by nature a special gift; if today his influence begins to make itself felt in the whole world, then it is a question of a quite new kind of power, reposing on spiritual and moral foundations: on, on an average, higher development of purely spiritual capacities, on thoroughly scientific knowledge, on the ranking of individuals in the framework of scientific methodology, on reliability, faith, all of which - as we have now become especially clearly aware in the war which sent us wasps and gnats - has done no damage to the old adventurer and daredevil. The still closer analysis of this special "mind" would lead too far here; let this one thing suffice: if the English bravery derives from world cruisers and pirates, the German thoroughness from the teacher: without the teacher, it would never have acquired development; the German elementary school teacher, the middle school teacher and the high school teacher not only achieved the victory of 1866 and 1870, he is generally the pioneer in the chain of victories of the German mind which has been commenced. If Germany too will at one time be a world conqueror, then it is the well-planned self-discipline which has enabled it to do this. Success became dangerous to the English mind - originally closely related to the German, in spite of all the wisdom of the present-day leading articles - it corrupted one thing and developed another too strongly. No reasonable, informed man will deny the presence of higher scientific talent in the English people; a hundred-year old politics has however in the mass of the people of all social ranks led to an unconditional neglect of the intellectual generally and therewith also of all science and all philosophically sober thought; only the immediately practical is valued, that which leads in the shortest way to independence and money. An English teacher of physics and chemistry narrated to me that all the boys commenced this subject of instruction recently introduced into some schools with mistrust, in that they asked, "Does it pay?," does it bring in money? One may consider what that must mean when fourteen year olds already think so! As soon, therefore - as it happens today - as science, and with it the mastery of the mind, gains more and more in significance in the economic machinery of the people, England may not keep pace and the rule of its world-empire would sink down to a declaration of brutal power. The day when Germany too will have organised its state machinery scientifically the superiority of England will be over. The English themselves know very well how it stands: not the efficiency of the state, only the will power of the whole and the efficiency which still predominates in the people holds the colossus together. Before me lies an English essay - in manuscript, since such a thing would not be printed - which glaringly illuminates the growing inability of the English bureaucrats, their increasingly difficult task of being just, in their native country and outside; chaos, which recently became suddenly public in the case of the arms-supplies, rules, as was demonstrated here, in all fields of the fully unsystematic, wildly fortuitously arisen authority that can be supervised by no man. And then let one begin the introduction to that "analysis" which I recommended previously. The anonymous author, who speaks from lifelong experience as a parliamentary official, shows here in detail that the English Parliament - held before us always as an unequalled model - after it has seized all power for itself, now shows itself increasingly incapable of fulfilling its tasks. Anyone who reads these fifty pages discovers that the whole amounts to a caricature: most important laws - for example, hygienically indispensable ones - stand for thirty years on the programme, without ever coming to a settlement before loud "political" debates; legal notions whose precise definition would be indispensable for the judge have been waiting a hundred years for this definition, and, in the meantime, vice and crime go free all round; in order to propagate at least the most indispensable ones and not leave the state machine to come entirely to a standstill, the government brings in, instead of new, pressingly necessary laws, small amendments and changes to old and outdated laws, which then slip through unnoticed, which, however, leads to a bad patchwork of unrelated items. "The incompetence of Parliament," says our expert, "is more than a curiosity, it is a disaster." Thither leads inevitably each pure parliamentary government; if it comes to the Revolutionary ideal, then is the chaos complete.

In the essay *Die Zuversicht*,[188] 1 recently quoted lines which I had received in November 1914 from a man who stands at the centre of the political life of Germany.[189] Here I would like now to transcribe a longer fragment from a letter which I myself wrote twelve years earlier - in November 1902 - to this personality. The opposition between England and Germany in relation to their kind of political organisation especially deserves to be apprehended still more sharply and the epistolary lends immediate freshness to the arguments. Besides, the complaint will often be raised against me, as against other participants in the present movement of minds, that we suffer from a pathological over-excitement produced by the war, a "*morbus bellicosus.*" The citation from the letter - which I bring forward almost *verbatim* - then, at least shows that the concerned sickness flourished chronically in me even in peace time.

"In my opinion, the entire programme for Germany's future lies in Goethe's words - externally limited, inwardly unlimited. Germany is destined - or we may say, would be destined - to become the heart of mankind! Every other people is now definitely ruled out; either Germany will be it, or we will be dissolved into a heartless chaos, into the original mash of character longed for by the Bishop of Ripon.[190] But the world is now large; the heart must therefore be a powerful one which labors flawlessly. Concentration and organisation (condensation and working out): in these two words lies Germany's future - if it wants to have one. Never will Teutonism be able to compete with Anglo-Saxonism through the method of the uniting of individuals into

---

188 [H.S. Chamberlain, *Die Zuversicht*, München: F. Bruckmann, 1915, Vol. II].
189 [Kaiser Wilhelm II, with whom Chamberlain maintained a correspondence; see Chamberlain, *Briefe 1882-1924 und Briefwechsel mit Kaiser Wilhelm II,* ed. P. Pretzsch, 2 vols., München: F. Bruckmann, 1928].
190 The well-known English preacher, also esteemed in Germany, had, at that time, recently expressed his ideal of a world peace through a mixture of all peoples and races.

atomic efficiency: in the German people too much Slavic blood circulates, and behind both peoples lies a too anomalously shaping historic development. Such an atomism (brilliantly as it may have succeeded over there, too) is as little to be wished for for Germany as the corresponding Utilitarianism in philosophy would be an advantage for the German intellectual culture. For that which he calls freedom - that which he in the time of his absolute monarchs, of a Henry VIII, of an Elizabeth, possessed in such an excellent measure - the Englishman had to sacrifice inner freedom; he has now become a will-less herd animal of whom a pair of newspapers and a handful of politicians make what they will; a crown which protects his freedom does not exist any more, for it is hopelessly enfeebled and henceforth hardly anything more than a headdress. At the same time England is on the point of losing its culture in the wild battle of atoms. Once England was the mother of universities; in the Oxford of the 13th century individual teachers had so many thousands of listeners that they had to give their lectures in the open-air; England at that time supplied the whole of Europe with scholars. Today, the matter stands, according to the last statistics, in the following manner: in Germany one man in 213 attends high school and therefore receives to a greater degree than otherwise possible the capacity for a real culture of the spirit; in England only one man in 5000 can allow himself this luxury, and if one brought in the preponderating number of Anglican theologians into the calculation - whose cramming of a few Hebraic scraps and of outdated theological formulisms would not be called high-school culture at all - then the proportion would emerge as a still more largely unfavorable one and amounts to, certainly not one man in 10000, perhaps hardly one in 20000. Yet, education alone does not do it; it is of course a national property, but, in and for itself, it constitutes no national power to be made use of politically; in addition to this, education must be organised and must penetrate all layers from top to bottom. About this an outstanding English expert, Professor Dewar,[191] as president of this year's convention of the British Association,[192] has recently spoken highly noteworthy words. After he has argued that the German chemists are 'two generations ahead' of the English, whereby it is made clear that Germany increasingly establishes the monopoly of the chemical industry, he continues: 'In my opinion it is not however the

---

191 [Sir James Dewar (1842-1923). See his "Presidential Address to the British Association, 1902" in *Collected Papers of Sir James Dewar,* ed. Lady Dewar, Cambridge, Cambridge Univ. Press, 1927, Vol.11, p.765-7].

192 This corresponds approximately to the annual conference of German doctors and natural scientists.

fact that the Germans seize this and that industry that really induces fear but rather that Germany today possesses a national weapon of precision which must straight away provide it with enormous advantages in each and every battle in which disciplined and methodically schooled intellectual powers come into play'. So speaks a sober judicious chemist! And how right he is! I believe that disciplined and methodically schooled intellectual powers will gain victory in every battle, in the battle of the peoples not less than in that of the chemical factories; only, the intellectual efficiency - as it happened in the case of the army - must naturally be trained actually to discipline and the politics led by the spirit of science must understand to forge a weapon of precision out of it.

We have reached today a turning point of world history. Never, as far back as history may look, has an even similar world situation prevailed; how then should the old organisations have held out? We need new political principles. The Anglo-Saxon has made the matter as simple as possible for himself in that he, as long as it went well, adapted the old to the new; that is 'happy-go-lucky' work. Our new age is however the work of science (including technology) and it is science which will rule them - as soon as it wishes. Not, by no means, not! the philosopher, as our noble Plato wished, but the nation drilled to scientific politics and, therefore, dealing according to plan and well-disciplined. This way - that of the increasing complication of the organised whole and of the growing subordination of the isolated individual under the whole - does entire Nature show us, in opposition to the fine phrases of the Revolution and to that political dilettantism which calls itself Liberalism.[193] It may not correspond to sentimental dreams; it however - in the case of the foundations of the Germans - alone leads to success. On all the paths of the new life developing around us we see that, more and more, time-saving and the simplification of means are striven for. The straight line is the shortest way between two points: this old truth emerges now for the first time as legislative also in the field of practical life; for, in the case of the highly developed quality of this life, in the case of the thousand claims which approach us, in the case of the increasing amount of things worth knowing, it is impossible that we may manage it if we do not bear it in mind. Here we may notice just one difference: to a given goal the Anglo-Saxon simplifies, [194] whereas the German reduces. [195] The

---

193 [cf. Paul de Lagarde's attack on Liberalism in his essay "Die graue Internationale", *Deutsche Schriften*, Göttingen, 1886, pp.399-414].
194 [simplifiziert].
195 [vereinfacht].

Anglo-Saxon, that is, saves time for himself for the practical life, in that he sacrifices his culture; the German, on the other hand, must save time for the culture of the mind, in that he shapes the political methods scientifically-summarily and thereby succeeds in accomplishing a longer way in a shorter time in the case of state businesses. To the true organic subordination of the individual - the polar opposite of slavery - belongs a higher culture than the English system demands or even just allows. Germany can outstrip Anglo-Americanism only by the fact that it follows a fully opposite political method and emerges as a closed unity - disciplined and methodized, as our good Dewar rightly says. Germany - I am strongly convinced of it - can within two centuries succeed in ruling the entire globe (in part directly politically, in part indirectly through its language, methods, culture), if - yes, if - it only succeeds in entering the 'new course', and that means, in bringing the nation to a definite break with the Anglo-American government methods and with the state-destroying ideals of the Revolution. The freedom which Germany needs is freedom as Frederick understood it - unlimited freedom of thought, of science, of religion - not freedom to rule badly as one likes.

No better formula for this political ideal would I know of than Goethe's "externally limited, inwardly unlimited"; after every turn that way it must become a password. If it would, then no numbers would frighten me. A race-conscious Germany - excluding everything un-German from the government and from its deliberations - organised politically uniformly from the center to the extremities, conscious of its goal (whereby the special characters and morals and constitutions of the different races would have to be observed and fostered), even if less affluent in the number of its inhabitants than the Anglo-Saxons and Russians, would nevertheless rule the world through external might and through inner elevation of spirit at the same time."

Thus far my letter of the year 1902.

If one asked me how I conceive this new political organisation on scientific principles, then I answer with the original cultivator: I warn of the way which lures to the abyss, I point out the way which leads to another blessed land - one cannot demand more of me; I am no dreamer; what no eye glimpses no man can describe. If, nevertheless, some suggestions of that which will emanate only from the wisdom of man "as nature" - it can indeed be a matter only of the shadows of coming things - should be obtained, then I must descend a step from the standpoint of purely objective observation hitherto observed and allow a subjective element to mix itself in. This will occur in the following last section.

V

Man should not look into his future condition,
but have faith in himself.

Herder

Admiral Mahan, the author of the well-known work, *The Influence of Sea Power upon History,*[196] as well as of other professional scientific books, once writes: "As regards the acquired ability to design an organisation according to plan and to enroll itself in it, Germany is at the head of all nations."[197] These words of the esteemed American officer, politician, and historian I introduce here because I am often represented by honest and dishonest enemies as a dreamer and enthusiast - which I am indeed not, for I suffer rather under an inborn inclination, and one further strengthened and directed through a natural-scientific course of education, towards pedantically certain knowledge of facts, on account of which I work troublesomely long; but what does one wish to undertake in this world against "fables convenues"?[198] Now, of Mahan no man will dare to maintain that he is not a learned expert on recent history, that he is not a practical, worldly-wise man versed in political questions, so little will any one be able to maintain that he is predisposed by his party in favor of Germany, since his sympathies belong manifestly to England and he does not fear for his own fatherland any more than any step which might induce England and Germany into an alliance. And this sober practical man judges, as one sees, exactly as I do. Indeed, he says something more,

196 [Alfred Thayer Mahan, *The influence of sea power upon history,* Boston: Little, Brown, 1903].
197 Cf. *The interest of America in international conditions,* London, 1910, p. 101.
198 accepted fables.

which gives evidence of the deepest insight: that it is significant for Prussia, "that it let itself be plastically modelled by a strong government, without the individual forfeiting the power of initiative in the circle of activity peculiar to him." Thereby is the point of departure of the new political ideal given: for, a nation of drilled machines would be morally worthless and could correspond only for a short time to the demands of life; a nation, on the other hand, which adapts itself to a generally plastic shaping and thereby remains freely creative nevertheless in all its individual parts: such a nation is like one of the living beings created by Nature and is, unlike any other hitherto, apt to grow into a real organism of unheard of efficiency; its downfall is not to be anticipated. Of the things which led me to Germany, Mahan certainly knows little, perhaps nothing; questions of practical politics make up his circle of interests, especially including the conduct of the war; he has however learnt also in this way to obtain a profound insight which has discovered to him exactly the same thing which a thirty year long occupation with the German spirit on its highest elevations revealed to me! That should give the reader confidence and encourage him to live within the idea to which this small work is dedicated and to comprehend it in its full significance.

Anyone who has read observantly and repeatedly until now will, I believe, find that, gradually, from negation and affirmation many positive results have been obtained, important principles, or - as the German language finely expresses it - basic axioms, that is, earthen walls and pillars to build a new building. Until now I hold what has been said as scientifically irrefutable; what follows now expresses a few things which I believe I myself may conclude, whereby, however, I do not take it upon myself to anticipate - not even in thought - man "as Nature." One asks, I answer; and indeed I answer only because I think that, in the case of some points of this supplement, understanding of what has preceded, and therefore also confidence in it, will be increased.

In one respect I do not believe in essential changes: namely, in respect of the general geographical-political composition of the German Reich; affiliations and thereby perhaps here and there the emergence of a new unity are possible, they would enrich the entire picture, yet change little of it; the hoped-for comprehensive formation of a union of states (of which I could not speak in *Deutscher Friede)*[199] would have certainly much to signify even inwardly as a strengthening of Germany, but it belongs however - as regards our subject - to the

---

199 [See H.S. Chamberlain, "Deutscher Friede" in *Neue Kriegsaufsätze*, München: F. Bruckmann, 1915].

external circumstances; even colonial possessions are worth less to me than, for example, the hoped for enlargement of the German peasantry; Germany's rebirth can succeed only from inside. No country in the world however has ever possessed in this respect more striking preconditions for a rich organic state life as Germany today: united and yet consisting of independent parts. What was hitherto Germany's curse - its manifoldness - has now become its blessing. For, the history of Europe has taught us: monarchy embodies indeed the greatest political power, if it however turns into absolute despotism, then it ossifies and is either swept out by demagogy (France) or it serves the latter as a protective shield (present day England). Plato has already taught us: Unity must include an opposite, otherwise we will not become aware of it even as a unity! In the entire realm of Nature, multiplicity belongs precisely to organic life, on account of which also, in those organs and structures whose essence it is not to occur twofold or fourfold but once, always some sort of difference - and even if it be only between a left and a right - is discovered through closer observation, mostly however an (often hidden) doubling or indeed multiplying -for which I refer to the discoveries of the last thirty-five years in relation to the structure of nuclei, which one might have considered as strict examples of indivisible unity. The multiplicity of the Reich and of the principalities in Germany is a divine blessing; thereby is, the kingship protected from the French and from the English entombing. The Kaiser in Goethe's *Faust* indeed means it differently when he cries out:

> A counter-king is an advantage to me:
> Now I feel for the first time that I am a king.[200]

Precisely this place however opened my eyes years ago and I perceived henceforth: a prince is no prince. The poor lonely person of Buckingham Palace or Czarskoje Selo[201] is in all cases - whether autocrat or constitutional costume-king - given up to his circumstances; in the entire kingdom he finds neither his equal for support and profit nor levels at which good minds could change and vary in order to unite him with the nobility and the people; he lives within a bell-jar: around him the void. The multiplicity of the "uniform" monarchy, if first formed organically - for which the preconditions are given in Germany today - means the living and lasting influence of the monarchy. If the blood circulates more energetically in all the parts of Germany than in any other country, that happens then because it does not possess a

---

200 [Faust, Part II, Act IV, 'Auf dem Vorgebirg'].
201 [The summer residence of the sovereigns of Russia, about thirty miles from Petersburg].

centre but many centres, not one court but many courts, not a monotonous uniformity of state resembling itself everywhere, but a multiplicity of branches strongly anchored in their own state structures, their own loyalty to the prince, their own manners, their own institutions of all sorts, calling forth noble contests. Of the heirlooms of France - the Revolution took it over from the degenerate royalty and cried it out as a dogma to the entire world - nothing is more disastrous than the demand of logical unity, the sameness which begins in the great and finally spreads into the smallest, producing awfully empty "equality." To Germany has been gifted by fate the advantage of manifold unity; it must learn to preserve it and to cultivate it. Here I think of no other change than that - to be sure, very important - of a development to a stronger participation of the Areopagus[202] of princes in the government of the Reich; that will strengthen the kingship and instil new life into the monarchic principle; every structure grows with the demands.

On the other hand, I believe, as regards the inner constitution, in the case of such a thorough transformation, that the French Revolution will in comparison appear as a game of vicious boys, as an external destruction without any trace of inner creativity. The German Revolution - if one wishes to say so, I prefer "renaissance" - will have to succeed from inside, so that where even an old thing falls a new stands there perfectly completed: that is the method of organic nature. For this reason is it indispensable, if we speak also of political ideals and their practical realization, to grasp the questions here always not from considerations of external viewpoints, but from the innermost kernel, from the nature of man, from the notion of duties which bind us to one another. Because this does not happen with it, for that reason does the present day Socialism operate unsatisfactorily and provoke a contradiction; to be sure, one feels that the genuine power of man "as Nature" stirs here, but every question is grasped for a false purpose, everything from outside, which is basically un-German, and therefore also fruitless in Germany. And yet Germany has borne the greatest revolutionary of all times, the man destined to light the way, as a leader, to the German world into the new formation of the life of the state: Immanuel Kant.[203] "To protect freedom": that did this gifted and really so little understood wise man point out as the highest goal - truly a different spiritual and moral power from a Marx or a Lassalle! But he

---

202 [The *Areopagus* was the Athenian political council].

203 Of the following some things are borrowed *verbatim* from my book published in 1906, *Immanuel Kant, die Persönlichkeit als Einführung in das Werk.* (Popular edition, 1909).

does not conceive it, as the French, from outside, as if one could pluck freedom like an apple from the tree, for he knows that: "Freedom is the work of man"; freedom is an idea of the human spirit; it can bring evil or distribute blessings; apart from mankind the whole of Nature knows nothing of freedom; the idea of a universal freedom - in opposition to the self-willed disorder of the individual - is therefore not a given reality, something to which every man has a claim; rather, Nature and freedom are in immediate opposition in the given reality, which each individual may know from his own experience, and as all history teaches; this idea represents something which should be first created and which alone may create the whole as ordered into a state: the last, highest, most difficult to reach, goal of the state. It is a question, says Kant, in his penetrating fashion, "of a kingdom which is not present but can become real through our actions and abstinences." The first step to this "only possible" but, as soon as we wish, real kingdom consists in the insight that the present situation is untenable: in this Kant is fully one with the so-called "revolutionary parties." Kant, who lived through the beginning of the Industrial Age and was especially precisely informed of English situations - the much praised - minted for them the famous phrase, "shining misery" and judged the modern state, in which the business interests were considered as decisive: "One may say that the happiness of states grows simultaneously with the misery of the people." In a few words the most bitter criticism indeed that has ever been addressed to the jubilation over "shining export and import balances" which has in the meantime grown so familiar to us. For the understanding of the new, coming political ideal - of the German ideal of the state - it is of decisive importance to perceive that: criticism of the external structure does not operate decisively (as was the case in France and in England) in a political transformation; rather all the wisest Germans will say here with Goethe: "I may let myself gladly be governed and taxed, if only one let the sun in through the opening of my barrel";[204] decisive are the inner conditions. It belongs to the nature of all the more noble Germans that a strong feeling for the dignity of man fills them. This feeling necessarily presses from the individual further to the whole and to the universal; for, how should dignity exist near indignity? Every individual man in the entire state must therefore possess the dignity in which freedom and the other properties lie included: that is the German demand. And then we perceive there that it does not suffice that the sun shine in the opening of one's barrel for this person or that; if it does not seem so to every citizen, then is that happiness a robbery; and therefore - therefore, from this inner basis of

---

204 [See Goethe's letter to Georg Sartorius, mid-January, 1815].

the moral law - the present state must be transformed from inside and born anew. "Man," writes Kant, "must either work himself or others for him; and this work will rob others of as much of their happiness as he wishes to raise his own [happiness] above the average"; our present state is, on the other hand, for the most part, aimed at the protection and assistance of him who - according to the Old Testament saying -wishes to be happy without any real work. Richard Wagner expressed it clearly shortly before his death: "Who can look throughout one's life with open senses and a free heart at this world of murder and robbery organised and legalised through lies, deception, and hypocrisy, without at times having to turn away in shuddering disgust from it?"[205] I said that the state has to consider only the duration not the individual: from this principle it must be inferred; the state may not inquire after the wishes of the individual, but must be established in itself as the expression of a whole destined to last; for, only a strong state is capable of sufficing for its goal. If however man, in the blessing of the state sheltering him, has grown spiritually and morally, then the state must also grow, that is, grow in its demands on itself; otherwise, there will be an end of its duration and it will not correspond any longer to its life goals; and what must be demanded, that has Kant brought into a sentence which at first may sound strange - especially to ears accustomed to our usual political phrases - but which operates invincibly, like the hammer of Thor, under whose weight an entire world of lies collapses: in a state there may not be a single man who does not "act at every time as a goal, never merely as a means." That is: no man may worry about another man's will, without this worrying assisting himself too - him as a being with a share in living, moral, intellectual and eternal possessions. He can indeed be a "means" - every one who serves and who does not serve is this, from the King to the stone cutter - but this serving may not forget for a moment that every individual is a "self-goal"; the state should make it impossible that a part of the citizens subjugate another part in that it reduces it to a mere "means," as if these men were mere machines and did not possess the God-given dignity of immortal souls. The four hundred thousand slaves who created the leisure for the twenty thousand Athenians and their Socrates to politicize in the *agora* and to philosophize in the shadows of plane trees were a mere "means" thereto, they lived no "goal" of their own, therefore did not enjoy the dignity of men. The six-year-old boys who must today in the pride-free democratic republic of the United States work for twelve hours are only a "means" for the masters of the factories who look out for cheaper

---

205 [Richard Wagner, "Das Bühnenweihfestspiel in Bayreuth"; see *Prose Works*, tr. W.A. Ellis, Vol.VI, p.312].

labour force; they mostly die before adulthood, or reach it embittered, crassly ignorant, demoralized; that they possess dignity as men, that they themselves should be a "goal," that it therefore would be an imperative duty to take care of these children, educate and allow them to take part in what mankind has achieved in the course of centuries, of that the people of the democratic Revolutionary ideal do not think; for such thoughts there is no place in the creed of materialism; the "freedom" which is so loudly glorified is the freedom to enslave men; the only question runs: do you enslave me? or do I enslave you? Brutal power gives the answer. Kant however forbade not only that a man use another as a "means," but that man may not use even himself so, may not live in such a way that his existence remains without a higher content, and he himself without dignity, rather must he, in everything that he does, reach out beyond his limited ego and its interests into the surrounding welfare of the community and into the presentiment of the immortal significance of our earthly activity and life. To use a personality - no matter if it be one's own or another's - merely as a means to the acquisition of a fleeting, egoistic goal, and not as one which itself represents in each and every one of its activities an unconditional sacred goal: that is the sin, that alone. "Man is indeed sufficiently unholy, but the humanity in his person must be holy to him."

I seem to wander, but am quite within the subject. According to my conviction, in the work of this man is fixed the greatest revolutionary power of world history; he himself, the modest man, confesses that his world-view steers towards a revolution, against which the hitherto externally political ones shrink to negligible episodes; Kant wishes to realize new ideals, not however through enthusiasm and philosophical dreaming, but through the soberly conscious change, effected slowly but surely with irresistible power in the back-room of the quiet thinker, with regard to human thought and will. In religion Jesus Christ brought in a new era; in politics, on the other hand, we have for 6000 years made no fundamental progress; when recently the ancient Hammurabi law tablets were discovered, they struck us as astonishingly modern; Kant on the other hand wants a new man, a growth and strengthening of man beyond that which he has been until now, not perhaps through the lunatic unchaining of his blind "will to power" [206] but, on the contrary, through a finer formation of his self-consciousness, through the still more precise curbing of the foolish animal-like instincts of his will in the service of a perfectly self-mastered, consciously creating reason. Until now, he says, and no

---

206 [Chamberlain's snide reference to the philosophy of Nietzsche].

one will be able to contradict him, "culture" has "progressed without plan as it were"; now it is time to develop it further according to a plan. And if until now all culture was possible only in the state and under its wings then that will be the case more than ever now; for that reason must our politics henceforth become scientific and organic. That which has been presented now forms an inner reason; and the German demands to know the inner reasons of things. Rightly so: for how should he go forth to the creation of a new thing, to the building of a for the first time genuinely German politics, of a really organic state, if he does not also precisely understand and contemplate the inner impulses?

The question, therefore, which was posed at the end of the last section - how I think of the new political organisation, I answer above all with one word; "in a Kantian manner." Therewith two things are immediately declared, from which a thousand individual questions are answered by themselves: the unconditional moral foundation, and the conscious construction according to a plan (and that means a scientific-organic plan). The second will never succeed if the first remain unobserved.

An iron broom must sweep through Germany: one who has the courage to drive it will find all the power of the people behind him. We have to fear no puritanism in such an artistic and bright people; dirt however is not of German origin, but an importation from outside and bred by the same people who overspread the ancient Roman empire with their vicious obscenity and levelled it to the ground.[207] What sort of freedom is the freedom to disseminate lascivious books throughout the entire country or illustrated newspapers that drag everything genuine, everything noble, everything sacred, week after week, into the mud? And yet, every German government trembles before these rascals, because, as soon as they move a finger, a powerful part of the press cries out "Enough!" on account of the threatened business earnings of their customers and, if possible, even mobilizes a "Goethe federation" - as if the gifted poet were the patron saint of pornography, and as if he had not warned over and over again most sharply against "the sweet freedom of the press," and mocked it appositely:

> Everybody wishes himself so free,
> As to force others 'honestly'[208]

---

207 [cf. H.S. Chamberlain, *The Foundations of the nineteenth century*. Part I, Division II, 'Introductory', where he discusses the Syrian-Semitic elements that brought about the degeneration and downfall of Rome].

208 [*Fragments*, 'Epigrammatisch'. The first line originally reads "Jeder wünscht die Freiheit sich" (Everybody wishes freedom for himself)].

and solemnly reminded his German people:

> If you have lied in word and letter,
> It is a poison to others and to you.[209]

As long as faint-heartedness forms the guiding principle of all inner and external politics, nothing is surely to be hoped for here; a single leading article of the *Berliner Tagblatt* is worth more to many German statesmen than the voices of fifty million Germans; yet that is a transitional phenomenon; the new men stand ready. It was necessary for me only to stress that, without cleansing, no beginning of a renewal can be hoped for; and indeed the cleansing will have to be wide-ranging, for all of the wind is infected and involuntarily Goethe's prescient description of the modern metropolis comes into one's mind, when he lets the old man who has dwelt a long time in distant natural countries speak:

> O! that I had not returned, misled by a sincere
> Inclination to be useful to the fatherland,
> To this wilderness of saucy state life,
> To this desert of refined crime,
> To this cesspool of egotism.[210]

Hardly a stone of the new building is yet present - if we disregard the exemplary national army - and, already, the conspiracy against a new Germany, against a genuinely German politics and the transformations requisite for it is at work everywhere; in the midst of the war its insolent face peeps from a thousand corners and, after the war, it will directly dart forth presumptuously once again. Millions of good Germans know all this, are inconsolable about it, many discouraged to the point of despair; I have received hundreds of letters from men from different walks of life in the last week which prove it. Now! why does one not first grapple with the demanded denial here, where no political questions make men irresolutely wavering? A strong-fisted German revolt against the rule of the common people which has already subjugated all other countries, almost completely and threatens the existence of Germany as a healthy, free people and makes its political recovery impossible! Unconditional freedom of science is a costly possession; freedom of greed, freedom of betrayal, freedom of exploitation, freedom of anti-Christianism, freedom of reverence-destroying ideas in speech, word, and picture, in book,

---

209 [*Zahme Xenien,* II].
210 [*Die natürliche Tochter,* Act V, sc.7].

journal and newspaper, in theatre and cinema-hall is a consuming poison by which nations are destroyed; to guarantee freedom to the people who undermine our Germanic political ideals of today and of tomorrow simply means to commit suicide. No political renaissance can therefore begin as long as vulgarity in public life is allowed free and insolent and triumphant. A poor man who is driven by hunger to steal a loaf of bread with force goes into the correction-house; professional scoundrels become fabulously rich and receive in the best of cases an order. Francis Bacon adduces an ancient author in agreement who wrote: "It were better anyway to live in a state where nothing is allowed than in one where everything is."[211] One may not however practise any idolatry with the word "freedom" which then finally guarantees just protection to every meanness! The entire goal of the state is, indeed, to establish and to watch over even as externally the limits of rule, so inwardly the limits of freedom.

These words I write in the sense of Kant, who exasperatedly questions our present statecraft: "How can one make men happy if one cannot make them moral and wise?" It is a question, as one sees, not of philosophical subtleties, but of scientifically precise ascertainments and demands which confront the basic questions of the future state. The state certainly does right to preserve property; we spoke of it in the third section; that happens for the sake of the state, as a chief means to lend it duration, not because the individual has some mystical "right" to it or would gain in dignity thereby. With Kant we reach a higher stage: for, the possession, not of land and gold, but of morality and wisdom raises both - the individuals and the state; therefore must this property be far more strictly yet watched over and taken care of and protected than the other. In this respect we have to basically learn afresh - and, with us, our administration of justice. For I do not see how we should attain strength and talent for a new higher politics as long as a large and influential number of us have not acquired the insight that morality and wisdom suit not only the person but signify political keystones, in other words, that they have to form a lasting chief concern of the state. In an earlier section of this work I indicated as our present task to make the ground free for the intervention of man "as Nature," who would know already to build up the German state of the future, as soon as space for it is left to him: through the planned energetic cleansing of the public life, I believe, sufficient will be done in the main for this demand. If this life is

---

211 [Francis Bacon, *Apophthegms new and old,* 69: "Galba succeeded Nero, and his age being much despised, there was much licence and confusion in Rome. Whereupon a senator said in full senate; 'It were better live where nothing is lawful, than where all things are lawful'].

first pure and German, then will everything else emerge by itself,
through natural necessity.

From this ground now must, as Kant expressed it, be built up
"according to plan"; I had the same thing in mind when I said
"scientifically-organically"; it is a question of that which Admiral
Mahan called "Germany's capacity to outline organisation according to
plan and to involve itself in it." I must always repeat: only the dreamer
sketches ready-made buildings in this place, as if he knew how men
will solve the problem; the thoughtful man announces the necessity of
the new, admonishes and stimulates one to give oneself to this thought,
listens to the thousand voices which call for it, some in enraged denial,
others fantastically effusive, still others scientifically ponderous, some
for political, others for economic or religious regeneration, and in his
ears the hard dissonances are blended into the promising music of a
dawning, finer future; but he does not describe, because he would
thereby distort that which is approaching. Goethe - in spite of his
disinclination for abstract notions - one of the most subtle thinkers of all
time, interrupts himself in the attempted description of a form not yet
glimpsed:

> Yet I speak to deaf ears, for the word strives
> Only in vain to creatively embody forms.[212]

Without undertaking for ourselves an "embodiment," it is perhaps
possible to reveal once again some of the leading notions of the coming
plan:

Above all this: if parliamentary representation in its present
revolutionary shape must unconditionally fall because it loses every
capacity for action, as we have seen, then should the participation of all
in the life of the state not, for that reason, become a lesser one: on the
contrary, I think it is to me far more significant than hitherto - the true
work of a practical cooperation, instead of the stupid exercise of an
imaginary right. In the present procedure everything is appearance and
untruth; the supposed "right of self-determination of the people," and as
all the phrases go, amounts to hardly more than a farce. The farmer who
makes a pilgrimage into the city to grant his vote for Councillor of
Commerce Morgenstern or Baron Pumpernickel, fancies himself
endlessly important and believes himself entitled to all sorts of claims;
he is incapable of supervising the construction of the German state; he
does not know what is necessary inwardly, much less still what a wise
politics requires from outside; his vote has been obtained through

---

212 [*Faust*, II, Act III, 'Vor dem Palast des Menelas zu Sparta', 11.8691f.].

definite promises which refer to his limited circle of interests - perhaps the cheaper acquisition of artificial fertilizer - and which cost nothing either to the Baron or to the Councillor; now he holds his *do ut des*[213] in his hand and becomes impudent or shouts about betrayal. It is just as immoral as unreasonable to give a man rights without developed duties along with them, and besides, rights which he himself does not understand at all. Edmond About [214] describes somewhere the Frenchman who proudly whispers to himself in the morning when he catches a glimpse of himself while shaving: "There stands the twenty seven millionth part of the all powerful ruler, France!" You poor man - interjects About - do you not observe then that you glimpse at the same time a complete slave of the tyrannical majority? That is what emerges in the case of the rule of ballots: arrogance matched with servility. It would be a different matter if it came to disposing the entire people, as in the case of the army, so also for the duties of the government. If the man owes in his youth a proportionate part of his forces to military service, then he could in riper years be obliged to state service - each one according to his education and capacity. The form of performance will present itself if first the principle is established. Nowhere is the citizen today invested with jurisdiction and authority with so much and such good success as in Germany; even in the associations and unions, the inborn gift of organisation seems to have been demonstrated in many places; one pursues this promising trace. I point analogically to the acknowledged quite especially excellent performances of the reserve officers in this war, as, generally, to the excellent military characteristics of the supplementary reserve officers and of the new land troops: we observe from this that man grows with the demands made on him. If a hundred thousand men from all walks of life found themselves suited after a short preparation to the hard, responsible, dangerous military service, how should they not prove themselves capable of performing service to the state? At the same time, it would be a blessing to reduce in this way the number of professional state officials- a career that is unsatisfactory, uninspiring in the case of all lower officials - to a minimum. Each of us should have to perform state duties first; if he has in this way entered into a living contact with the organism sustaining us all and has proved himself in his place, only then would he obtain political rights. Anyone who cannot perform practical duties in the service of the state - no matter whether he be rich or poor, noble or not - he would not receive any right to participation in

---

213 'I owe you's.
214 [Edmond About (1828-85) was an author of fantastic and farcical literary works as well as of a couple of economic treatises].

the state businesses, also no ballot constituted in any way. Neither aristocracy nor democracy: practical probation in a state whose artful organism spreads through millions of veins everywhere under the binding cooperation of all grown-up, irreproachable, capable men.

To this is directly connected a second thought which would operate not less revolutionarily - or let us say regeneratively.

The division of labour is an idea obtained from the observation of Nature; high accomplishments are achieved only through it. For a long time has this principle been brought forward also in the theory of the state; we hear wonderful things of the "division or separation of powers." Especially Montesquieu has introduced this idea into the largest circle of educated people, since he believed that he glimpsed in the England of his time (the first half of the 18th century) the ideal "three-fold division" and described it eloquently in this example: puissance legislative, puissance executive, puissance de juger, legislative power, executive power, judiciary power.[215] The parliament promulgates the laws, the ministry performs it, the king names the irremovable judges who speak justice in his name: so did Montesquieu envisage the matter. As far as I know, this theory of the division of powers is highly esteemed by all teachers of justice; in reality it does not exist anywhere. The brilliant Seeley[216] showed already thirty years ago how little the English state corresponds to Montesquieu's idealisation. A negligibly small number of laws issues from the initiative of the parliament; almost all are the work of the ministry - the supposed "executive power" - whose chief activity is precisely the development of new laws and the improvement of old ones. To be sure, each law must be passed by the parliament, before it obtains legal force; yet, if one disregards individual laws exciting the passions and interests, which then indeed occupy the parliamentary representation often a year long and even often reach acceptance distorted and disfigured and robbed of their hoped-for influence, then the parliament presents so little interest in the real legislative activities that the ministers have to enforce the most indispensable ones with strain and trouble. The true life of the parliament is apprehended only through two things: the political interests of the party, whether it be to destroy the government or to maintain it, and the granting of money. The parliamentary representation mingles itself uninterruptedly precisely in the executive power. And can one really term the granting of money a "legislative

---

215 [See Montesquieu, *L'Esprit des Lois* (1748), Bk.XI, Ch.VI: 'De la constitution d'Angleterre'].

216 [John R. Seeley, the British historian and author of *The Expansion of England,* London: Macmillan, 1883].

function"? Teachers of political justice disavow this question. Only the executive power supervises the entire situation and can judge which tasks are necessary and how they are to be guarded: if parliamentary representation takes over the decision in this matter, then it arrogates to itself the actual executive power and destroys thereby the balance beneficial to the state. In reality, things are conducted in present day England in such a way that the legislative power, the executive power and the naming of judges lie in the same hands, namely, in those of the ministry; over against it stands an assembly whose majority for the time being receives all good things from the mercy of the ministry, whose minority however strives against one and all - no matter if it is reasonable or not - in the hope of inciting the public opinion gradually against those having power and so of obtaining majority itself and, with it, the enjoyment of an almost unlimited might. And, *nota bene,* in especially interesting cases - interesting from the standpoint of the political mess - the ministry reserves to itself, and to the parliament obedient to it, also the judiciary inquiry and decision, as recently once again in the case of the neat schemes of the Marconi Society, by which ministers who possessed disreputable connections with the stock-exchange used their secret knowledge of proposed contracts between the government and the Society in order to move - with the aid of the corresponding spread of false news [217] - splendid "residual businesses"; on such things a specially set up "parliamentary commission" adjudicates, and therefore appropriates to itself the "judiciary power," and indeed with the hardly unsuccessful intention of whitewashing its good friends and of blackening its enemies - in short, of judging unjustly. How far does all this lie from Montesquieu's ideal!

I believe now that the German state of the future will basically carry out the separation of powers demanded by the theorists - recognized as scientifically necessary - with the result that, for the first time in the history of mankind, the real judiciary will be detached as completely as possible from politics - from all, I mean, which we otherwise understand by politics and can briefly summarize as a hunt for power. What in the world demands more sobriety, more impartiality, more wisdom, more feeling of a sacred responsibility than the development of laws on behalf of the state? Instead of a universal parliamentary representation embracing everything under it, which is there for all and nothing and burdens and troubles the life of the nation with the unpleasant consanguinity of the professional politicians, I

217 [On this point, see the Report of the Select Committee: "We find no suggestion that any Member of Parliament — [was] responsible for the origination or dissemination of the rumors", in Frances Donaldson, *op.cit.,* p.296].

consider a broadly ramified organization which - as it happens everywhere in naturally formed life - elastically accommodates itself to every emergent case, in order to ascertain, collect and sort out from the entire country the needs, wishes, opinions of those affected directly and indirectly by the law, until a really expert insight is obtained which then again must be tested by men especially qualified for it from the viewpoint of the general needs of life of the entire state. The Council of Ministers represents the final authority. Under our present conditions such a procedure is excluded: the elections to the so-called parliamentary representation take place from the standpoints of the parties; politicians, not expert people tested in law, sit in council; the haggling between the parties begins immediately and the laws reach from compromise to compromise an arbitrary shape; all that is exactly the opposite of "according to plan" and "scientifically organic." If, however, that general practical participation in the life of the state exists, which was mentioned previously, then an interception and screening of facts, conditions, relations, will be effected - apart from all politics, so that finally a fully expert, objective picture of the requirements is obtained, which then will be elaborately developed by the smallest number of the most qualified experts, with the cooperation of the concerned executive departments of the centre, into the required law. This last advisory body I consider not as a single Imperial Parliament, but as a committee formed every time *ad hoc* which does not occur in the same composition twice, since for each particular matter the professionally competent people are searched out without any consideration of their special viewpoints or their walk of life, and, besides, each one is obliged to these time-consuming state affairs only according to a definite order of succession. There should be no "politics" in the present sense in the new Germany; in its place enters statecraft. And there one will do well to pick up once again the brilliant Napoleon's plan and conduct all councils with the exclusion of the public - as it moreover happens already today in the case of the Federal Council.[218] There is not wanting today opportunity to express oneself openly; it is forbidden to no one to announce his viewpoints openly; that, however, almost all the parliamentary speeches are delivered without success and aim at something other than the advancement of the business lying at hand, that belongs to the political network of lies that is spun around us and which must be torn apart; besides, it is revoltingly contradictory to grant influence to eloquence in the case of the resolution of political questions. Even our newspaper reports on the debates constitute a rankling evil, for, in their shameless distortion of

---

218 [Bundestag].

the truth, they are calculated only to incite the passions and to reduce the power of judgement. On the other hand, as soon as elected professional delegates deliberate in a completely undisturbed manner, the best will, in a short time and in a perfect form, be performed for the welfare of the citizens who pursue in the meantime their own affairs.

Meanwhile the "executive power," consisting of a few officials and numerous citizens, will manage their office at all levels of its influence quickly, expertly, energetically and quietly. As was indicated already a little before, here Germany has during the last forty years prepared very much; the first framework already stands ready. Just as I write this last section, a favorable fate brings to my hands a work - *Deutschland und der Weltkrieg* (ed. by Hintze, Meinecke, etc., Teubner, 1915)[219] - which, constituted of very different parts, offers a henceforth indispensable collection of well-winnowed facts and contains some pleasant sections; one of the best is the essay of Dr. Hans Luther: *Das deutsche Staatsbürgertum und seine Leistungen in der Selbstverwaltung',* I urgently recommend every one of my readers to study it. "In no other country," writes Dr. Luther, "are the interrelations between the state and the individual worked out with so many rights and so much real influence on public life as in the German Reich."[220] Of special interest is the observation that, within the many free administrative bodies, the otherwise all-ruling political viewpoints are mostly dropped. Of the administrative deputations, "the most brilliant institution of the German political constitution," I know from the experience of my own Berliner friends that Conservatives and Socialists carry out the management of their tasks in complete harmony, and therefore make their decisions very fast and always professionally correctly. One needs only to develop further to a greater stage this genuinely German tendency to methodical organisation which is linked to ancient traditions, and the "self-administration" described here by Luther will encompass the entire Reich - the Reich of a people worthy of true freedom.

Even the "judiciary power" has already entered the right way in Germany, even if much still remains to be done.

Paul de Lagarde, whom we must revere as the complementary political genius to Bismarck - for, as the one showed the way of the present, so the other did of the future - said once: "A people is free only if it consists of true masters ... of masters down to the lowest strata of the nation."[221] Lagarde's thought comes to my mind during this

---

219 [see above p.96n.).
220 [*op.cit.,* p.220].
221 [Paul de Lagarde, *Über die gegenwärtige Lage des deutschen Reichs,*

tentative attempt to divine the future shape of the state. In the German national army every soldier is the comrade of the other, the youngest recruit that of the highest commander-in-chief; the structure makes up a family; what makes everyone equal is the obligation until death and to the service dedicated to the same goal. In the present formation of the political life such a fraternization cannot come about: the strata differentiated by fortune and family history stand alien to one another, often hostile to one another, the followers of the different political parties combat one another recklessly, those who profess different Christian creeds foster bitter feelings against one another. I think that the two indicated directions of action: the one towards a participation in the life of the state which becomes ever more universal, the other towards the elimination of politics in favor of one scientifically planned, will contribute much to comradely union. In a through and through organised state there will be no place for conspirators and intriguers; and merciless strictness against possible disturbers of the peace of the state will meet no resistance, where all efficient men are themselves involved in the being of the state. Today for many - perhaps for most - the state is a sort of hostile, at the least an alien, power which one sets oneself against either openly or secretly, and to scold which one does not let pass a single opportunity; even in the officials this alienation is reflected only too often through haughtiness, rudeness, sometimes even animosity. Down to these smallest details does the observing eye discover proofs of the unnaturalness of our political conditions: we drag around with us even thousand year old formulae and forms, whereby it is impossible that we may fare well. As little as I can with my weak eyes glimpse the shape of the coming state, so clearly do I glimpse the contempt with which our disgust will look back at us, as at clumsy fools. The state in which everyone has his definite, regulated duties - not to chat about and assess things and overthrow majority decisions, but to settle according to instruction, and, if supreme efficiency has been practically confirmed, to perfect with insight - this state will not be felt as a foreign body. One looks around oneself in the literature of the past century, with what feelings the army of mercenaries was considered; today the national army is the pride and joy of every good man. In Scharnhorst's sketch the first paragraph reads: "All the inhabitants of the state are born defenders of the same";[222] and the new principle is

---

Göttingen, 1875; rpt. in *Deutsche Schriften,* Gottingen, 1886, p.159].
222 [Gerhard von Scharnhorst (1755-1813) - Prussian army commander and military theorist - *Vorläufige Entwurf der Verfassung der Reservearmee* (August 1807), Art.l, in G. von Scharnhorst, *Ausgewählte militärische Schriften, ed.* H. Uszeck, C. Gudzent, Berlin Militärverlag der DDR, 1986, p.236].

immediately set out: "In peace only knowledge and education, in war only outstanding bravery and prudence guarantee a claim to officer positions." To the idiots who complain about German militarism, it is to be replied that this notion possesses no meaning any more, especially in Germany; in the army stands the first great section of the new state, the bulwark of German freedom - namely, in order that Germany will be "free" to raise its ideal of a cultured state within a hostile world fallen to barbarism. Without the army, without this great union of sacredly serious comradeship, of unquestioning subordination of all, unconcerned about situation, as about political and ecclesiastical denomination, all this would be already lost today. The state in its present constitution is not worthy of this army; the army and the state stand beside each other inharmoniously. The incomparably greater efficiency of the army administration, even in questions of the life of the citizens, has made a great impression during this present war and opened the eyes of many; often one hears the call: "Ah, if it could only remain this way after the war! Why should martial law not be proclaimed continuously against baseness and profiteering?" We saw at work here the "reduction" mentioned in the previous section and felt it as a blessing which - developed further - would free the nation from an enormous vice, as well as from an exhausting chronic agitation. It was, as if one gazed - as if illuminated by a flash of lightning - from night and chaos and labyrinthine pathlessness into reasonable possibilities.

Goethe once said that what men call freedom is nothing other than "disorderly self-will"; he was right; however, we say with Kant: "There is a kingdom which does not yet exist, but can be realised through our actions"; there, there will rule, instead of confusion, truth; instead of capriciousness, planned order; brotherhood will resemble the comradeship of the national army, where no one will desert the other; equality will comprise the strict proportionality of rights to fulfilled duties, that is, in the equal burdening of the two scales; and freedom will constitute the inner meaning and enjoyment – the unlimited – of a life conducted externally in a harmonious manner and strictly towards common goals, that is, of a life wisely limited.

Bayreuth, 31 July 1915.

Bibliography

Ia. The major works of Houston Stewart Chamberlain[223]

Das Drama Richard Wagners, Leipzig: Breitkopf und Härtel, 1892.
Richard Wagner. Echte Briefe an Ferdinand Praeger, Leipzig, 1894.
Recherches sur la sève ascendante, Neuchâtel: Attinger, 1897.
Die Grundlagen des neunzehnten Jahrhunderts, München: F. Bruckmann, 1899.
Parsifal-Märchen, München: F. Bruckmann, 1900.
Vorwort und Nachträge zur dritten Auflage der Grundlagen des XIX. Jahrhunderts, München: F. Bruckmann, 1901.
Worte Christi, München: F. Bruckmann, 1901.
Drei Bühnendichtungen, München: F. Bruckmann, 1902.
Dilettantismus. Rasse. Monotheismus. Rom. Vorwort zur 4. Auflage der Grundlagen des XIX. Jahrhunderts. München: F. Bruckmann, 1903.
Heinrich vom Stein und seine Weltanschaaung, Leipzig u. Berlin, 1903 (with Friedrich Poske).
Immanuel Kant. Die Persönlichkeit als Einführung in das Werk, München: F. Bruckmann, 1905.
Arische Weltanschauung, Berlin, 1905.
Wehr und Gegenwehr. Vorworte zur dritten und zur vierten Auflage der

---

223 This list includes only his books and not his numerous articles. For a detailed bibliography of Chamberlain's works, see G. Field, *Evangelist of Race: The Germanic vision of Houston Stewart Chamberlain,* N.Y.: Columbia Univ. Press, 1981.

Grundlagen des XIX. Jahrhunderts,
München; F. Bruckmann, 1912.
Goethe, München: F. Bruckmann, 1912.
Kriegsaufsätze ('Deutsche Friedenliebe', 'Deutsche Freiheit', 'Die deutsche Sprache', 'Deutschland als führender Weltstaat', 'England', 'Deutschland'), München: F. Bruckmann, 1914.
Neue Kriegsaufsätze ('Grundstimmungen in England und Frankreich', 'Wer hat den Krieg verschuldet?', 'Deutscher Friede'), München: F.Bruckmann, 1915.
Politische Ideale, München: F. Bruckmann, 1915.
Die Zuversicht, München: F. Bruckmann, 1915.
Deutschlands Kriegziel, Oldenburg, 1916.
Deutsches Wesen, München: F. Bruckmann, 1916.
Ideal und Macht, München: F. Bruckmann, 1916.
Hammer oder Amboss?, München: F. Bruckmann, 1916.
Democratie und Freiheit, München: F. Bruckmann, 1917.
Der Wille zum Sieg und andere Aufsätze, München: F. Bruckmann, 1918.
Lebenswege meines Denkens, München: F. Bruckmann; 1919.
Mensch und Gott: Betrachtungen über Religion und Christentum, München: F. Bruckmann, 1921.
Herr Hinkebeins Schädel: Gedankenhumoreske, München: F. Bruckmann, 1921.
Drei Vorworte, München: F. Bruckmann, 1923.
Rasse und Persönlichkeit, München: F. Bruckmann, 1925.
Natur und Leben (ed. J. v. Uexküll), München: F. Bruckmann, 1928.
Briefe 1882-1924 und Briefwechsel mit Kaiser Wilhelm II (ed. P. Pretzsch), München: F. Bruckmann, 1928.
Cosima Wagner und Houston Stewart Chamberlain im Briefwechsel 1888-1908, ed. P. Pretzsche, Leipzig, 1934.

1b. Translations

The Foundations of the Nineteenth Century, tr. J. Lees, London: John Lane, 1911.
The Ravings of a Renegade, being the War Essays of Houston Stewart Chamberlain, tr. C.H. Clarke, London: Jarrold and Sons, 1915.

II. Intellectual Relations

Arndt, E.M. *Arndts Ausgewählte Werke*, 16 vols. in 4, ed. H. Meisner, R.. Geerdes, Leipzig: Max Hesses Verlag, 1908.

le Bon, Gustave *La psychologie des foules*, Paris: F. Alcan, 1895.

La psychologie du socialisme, Paris: F. Alcan, 1898.

La Révolution française et la psychologie des révolutions, Paris: E. Flammarion, 1912.

La psychologie des temps nouveaux, Paris: E. Flammarion, 1920.

Fichte, J.G. *Sämtliche Werke*, ed. J.H. Fichte, Berlin: Veit und Co., 1845-46.

Addresses to the German Nation, tr. R.F.Jones, and G.H. Turnbull, Chicago: Open Court Publishing Co.,1922.

Popular Works, tr. William Smith, 2 vols., London:John Chapman, 1848.

The Science of Rights, tr. A.E. Kroeger, London: Trubner and Co., 1889, rpt. Routledge and Kegan Paul, 1970.

Gobineau, Arthur *Essai sur l'inégalité des races humaines*, Paris: P. Belford, 1967.

The inequality of human races, tr. A. Collins, N.Y.: H.Fertig, 1967.

Goethe, W. *Goethe: Berliner Ausgabe*, 23 vols., Berlin: Aufbau, 1972-78.

Herder, J.G. *Sämtliche Werke*, ed. B. Suphan, 33 vols., Berlin, 1877-1913.

Jung, Edgar Julius *Die Herrschaft der Minderwertigen*, Berlin: Verlag Deutsche Rundschau, 1930.

The Rule of the Inferiour, tr. A. Jacob, 2 vols. Lewiston, NY: The Edwin Mellen Press, 1995.

Kant, Immanuel *Political Writings*, tr. H.B. Nisbet, Cambridge: Cambridge Univ.Press, 1970.

Kant's Philosophy of Law, tr. W. Hastie, Edinburgh, 1887.

Lagarde, Paul de *Deutsche Schriften*, Jena: Eugen Diederichs, 1944.

Moeller van den Bruck, Arthur *Das dritte Reich*, Hamburg: Hanseatische Verlagsanstalt, 1923.

Germany's Third Empire, tr. E.O. Lorimer, London: George Allen and Unwin, 1934.

Rosenberg, Alfred *Blut und Ehre: Ein Kampf für deutsche Wiedergeburt*, ed. Thilo v. Trotha, München: Zentralverlag der NSDAP, 1934.

Gestaltung der Idee, ed. Thilo v. Trotha, München: Zentralverlag der NSDAP, 1936.

Der Mythus des zwanzigsten Jahrhunderts, München: Hoheneichen Verlag, 1939.

Die Spur des Juden im Wandel der Zeiten, München: Franz Eher

Nachfolger, 1939.

Selected Writings, ed. Robert Pois, London: Jonathan Cape, 1970.

Rousseau, Jacques *The Social Contract and Discourses*, tr. G.D.H. Cole, London: J.M. Dent, 1950.

Schiller, F. *Schillers Werke*, Weimar: Hermann Bohlaus Nachfolger, 1943-.

Spengler, Oswald *Der Untergang des Abendlandes: Umrisse einer Morphologie der Weltgeschichte*, München: Beck, 1920-22.

Decline of the West, tr. C.F. Atkinson, London: George Alien and Unwin, 1926.

Politische Schriften, München: C. Beck, 1934

Selected Essays, tr. D.O. White, Chicago: Henry Regnery Co.,1967.

Treitschke, H. von *Politics*, 2 vols., tr. A.J. Balfour, N.Y.: Macmillan Co., 1916, rpt. N.Y.: AMS Press 1978.

Selections from Treitschke's Lectures on Politics, tr. A.L.Gowans, London: Gowans and Gray, Ltd., 1914.

Wagner, Richard *Gesammelte Schriften und Dichtungen*, Leipzig: E.W. Fritsch, 1897-98.

Prose Works, tr. W.A. Ellis, London: Routledge and Kegan Paul, 1892-99.

III. Secondary Sources (This is a selected list.)

Biddiss, M.D. *Father of Racist Ideology: The Social and Political Thought of Count Gobineau*, London: Weidenfeld and Nicolson, 1970.

Butler, R. d'O. *The Roots of National Socialism*, 1783-1933, London, 1941.

Davis, H.W.C. *The Political Thought of Heinrich von Treitschke*, N.Y.: C. Scribner's Sons, 1915.

Dewey, John *German Philosophy and Politics*, N.Y.: Putnam, 1942.

Barnard, F.M. *Herder's social and political thought*, Oxford: Clarendon Press, 1965.

Bowen, R.H. *German theories of the corporative state*, N.Y.: McGraw-Hill Co., 1947.

Coker, F.W. *Organismic theories of the State*, N.Y.: Columbia Univ., 1910.

Engelbrecht, H.C. Johann *Gottllieb Fichte: A Study of his political writings with special reference to his nationalism*, N.Y.: Columbia

Univ. Press, 1933.

Favrat, J. *La pensée de Paul de Lagarde (1827-1891)*, Paris: Librairie Honorie Champion, 1979.

Field, G. *Evangelist of Race: The Germanic vision of Houston Stewart Chamberlain*, N.Y.: Columbia Univ. Press, 1981.

International Council for Philosophy and Humanistic Studies (ed.), *The Third Reich*, London: Weidenfeld and Nelson, 1955.

Jenschke, B. *Zur Kritik der konservativ-revolutionaren Ideologie in der Weimarer Republik: Weltanschauung und Politik bei Edgar Julius Jung*, München: Beck, 1971.

Klemperer, Klemens von *Germany's New Conservatism: Its history and dilemma in the twentieth century*, Princeton: Princeton Univ. Press, 1957.

Krieger, L. *The German idea of freedom: History of a political tradition*, Boston: Beacon Press, 1957.

Marriot, J.A.R. *Dictatorship and Democracy*, Oxford: Clarendon Press, 1935.

McGovern, W.M. *From Luther to Hitler: The History of Fascist-Nazi Political Philosophy*, Cambridge, Mass.: Houghton Mifflin Co., 1941.

Mendlewitsch, D. *Volk und Heil: Vordenker des Nationalsozialismus im 19. Jahrhundert*, Rheda-Wiedenbrück: Daedalus Verlag, 1988.

Mohler, Armin *Die konservative Revolution in Deutschland 1918-1932: Ein Handbuch*, Darmstadt: Wissenschaftliche Buchgesellschaft, 1972.

Mosse, George *The Crisis of German Ideology: Intellectual Origins of the Third Reich*, N.Y.: Grosset and Dunlap, 1964.

Odajnyk, W. *Jung and Politics: The political and social thought of C.G. Jung*, N.Y.: Harper and Row, 1976.

Pundt, A.G. *Arndt and the nationalist awakening in Germany*, N.Y.: Columbia Univ. Press, 1935.

Schuettinger, R.L. *The Conservative Tradition in European Thought*, N.Y.: G.P. Putnam's Sons, 1970.

Snyder, L.L. *From Bismarck to Hitler: The Background of modern German nationalism*, Williamsport: Bayard Press, 1935.

Sontheimer, K. *Antidemokratisches Denken in der Weimarer Republik: Die politischen Ideen des deutschen Nationalismus zwischen 1918 und 1933*, München: Nymphenburger Verlagshandlung, 1962.

Struve, W. *Elites against democracy*, Princeton: Princeton Univ. Press, 1973.

Stunner, M. *Das ruhelose Reich: Deutschland 1866-1918,* Berlin: Severin und Siedler, 1983.

Stutzinger, G. *Die politischen Anschauungen Houston Stewart Chamberlains,* Bottrop: W. Postberg, 1938.

Whisker, J.B. *The social, political and religious thought of Alfred Rosenberg: An Interpretive Essay,* Washington, D.C.: Univ. Press of America,1982.

Political law contradicts the laws of nature—
Nothing is more repulsive than the majority.

General Index